Air Force One

Air Force One

The Aircraft That Shaped the Modern Presidency

by Von Hardesty

Foreword by **Bob Schieffer**

See Air Force One!

By Bob Schieffer

AS THE WHITE HOUSE CORRESPONDENT for CBS News during the Ford and Carter presidencies, I traveled all over America and around the world many times on Air Force One. But I never understood the drawing power of the great blue and white plane until the fall of 1976, when I was covering Gerald Ford's presidential campaign.

We had landed at an airport in the Pacific Northwest. There was to be a brief rally there before we flew on to another stop. The crowd was larger than expected, and I soon realized why. As I made my way to an area that had been roped off for the press, I picked up a campaign flyer that had blown onto the tarmac. I was about to throw it into a trash bin when the headline caught my eye. Emblazoned in large type across the top of the sheet, it read, "Come See Air Force One." In smaller type, it noted that the president of the United States would also be making an appearance.

I told that story one day to retired U.S. Air Force Colonel Randall Larsen, one-time commander of the fleet of planes based at Andrews Air Force Base outside of Washington that are used to transport cabinet officers and ranking government officials. He laughed but wasn't surprised. Larsen grew up in Indiana in a neighborhood that

Opposite: With a wing span of nearly two hundred feet, Air Force One casts a huge shadow on the ground moments before landing in San Jose, California, on August 7, 1996.
Above: Bob Schieffer broadcasts a televised report in front of Air Force One at an airport in Bucharest, Romania, in 1975. President Ford met with the hard-line communist dictator Nicolae Ceausescu in an effort to encourage his independence from the Soviet Union.

bordered on the Indianapolis 500 racetrack, and he said that when he was thirteen years old his father learned that President Kennedy was coming there on a visit. "I'll never forget it," he told me. "My dad heard about it one day and said to me, 'Hey Randy, want to go see Air Force One?' I'm not sure he even mentioned that the president would be coming along. But he didn't need to; he knew what I would want to see was that airplane."

From 1996 to 1998, Larsen ran the 89th Airlift Wing at Andrews Air Force Base and was responsible for the forty-nine transports and helicopters in the VIP fleet — all of the VIP aircraft except the two big planes used routinely by the president. When he took formal command of the unit, the ceremony was held beneath the wing of Air Force One. "In my remarks, I said there were probably other colonels taking command of other units that day, but to stand there in the shadow of Air Force One, for me it was like winning at Indy," Larsen said.

Anyone who has traveled on Air Force One and watched the reactions that it evokes will understand what Larsen means. Air Force One has come to be as much a symbol of the American presidency as the White House.

Hamilton Jordan, who served as Jimmy Carter's White House chief of staff, calls it "the Presidency Plus" when the nation's chief executive arrives on Air Force One. "First there's that majestic plane," he said, "and then there's the entourage of Secret Service agents and military aides. It's like the circus coming to town or a celebrity you've seen on television or in the movies. People want to see how it all looks in person."

As America has grown larger and more diverse, television has become the one experience we have all shared, and as we have gathered around our TVs to watch the triumphs and tragedies of the last four decades, Air Force One has often been part of the picture. It was Air Force One that first came onto our screens when Richard Nixon made his historic visit to China, and it was from Air Force One that we saw John Kennedy's coffin lowered onto the airport tarmac after that awful day in Texas. Those scenes will be forever etched in the memories of the generations of Americans who saw them on television.

And there would be so many other pictures. In 1974, on a sunny morning at Andrews, I watched another unforgettable scene unfold at the door of Air Force One — a scene that would be broadcast around the world. Richard Nixon had been brought down by the Watergate scandal, and as he left Washington on that August morning, the last time Americans would see him while he still held the title of president was as he turned and entered the cabin of Air Force One. It was an eerie sight to behold, eerie because it all seemed so routine yet was anything but that. Nixon walked quickly up the steps to the cabin door as he always did, turned and waved and smiled as he always did. Yet the scene was not at all what it seemed. What we were seeing were the final scenes in one of the most traumatic periods in our nation's history. In a matter of hours, Nixon would be the first American president to resign the office.

He had said good-bye to the nation earlier that morning at the White House and had gone to Andrews for the flight home to California. By agreement, he was to officially give up the presidency at noon EST that day, but he was still president as the door of the plane closed, and because any plane on which the president rides carries the call sign Air Force One, it was Air Force One that ground controllers cleared for takeoff. But several hours later, as the plane flew west and noon approached, Nixon's pilot, Colonel Ralph Albertazzie, radioed the Kansas City Regional Flight Control Center and requested that his call sign be changed from Air Force One to SAM (Special Air Mission) 26000. At precisely the same time back in Washington, Gerald Ford was sworn in as the nation's first unelected president.

Some months later, I would witness yet another scene at the door of Air Force One that would indelibly mark the presidency of Nixon's successor. It was a misty day in Salzburg, Austria, and Ford had come there for talks with

Schieffer questions President Carter during a White House press conference in 1978. The longest trip he ever took with a president was on Carter's extended trip abroad in December 1977, when he made stops in Poland, Iran, India, Egypt, France, and Belgium.

Egyptian president Anwar el-Sadat. Ford was trying to renew efforts to forge yet another peace plan for the Middle East, but little is remembered from that day except what happened when Ford stepped out the door of Air Force One. As he gave an arm to his wife to help her down the steps, he slipped and fell headlong down the stairs and onto the concrete runway below. Those of us who were watching from the press area at first thought he had been shot. Miraculously, he was not hurt. But after that scene was broadcast around the world, Ford never recovered from the blow to his image he suffered that day. Comedians turned the incident into a running gag and as the joke went, Vice President Rockefeller was "only a banana peel away from the presidency." Ironically, Ford had been a college athlete and was in remarkable shape and health for a person his

age, but no politician is helped when he becomes the punch line of jokes. The pictures from that day — what Mrs. Ford later called "a stumbly, bumbly image" — dogged him throughout his presidency, and some of his advisors believed it was one reason he lost the election.

Every president of the television age has loved Air Force One and the mobility it brought to the presidency, and the atmosphere aboard the plane has always reflected each man's personality. For the reclusive Nixon, the compartment reserved for the president was a refuge, a place where he spent hours alone, developing and writing out on a yellow legal pad the early drafts of the ideas that would become the themes of his presidency. For Ford, the plane was a place to relax and unwind, and other passengers on board reflected Ford's informality. Most of the reporters

Walter Cronkite, Bob Schieffer, and Eric Severeid interview President Ford in the White House for a prime-time television program in 1975. Before the interview, Schieffer's mother told him to be respectful. Schieffer told her he was always respectful to the president. "I meant toward Mr. Cronkite and Mr. Severeid," his mother replied. President Ford soon heard the story, and he wrote Schieffer's mother to reassure her that Schieffer had been respectful to all three of them.

who travel with a president fly aboard a chartered commercial airliner, but a half dozen, called the "press pool," ride aboard Air Force One to report what happens there to the rest of the press corps. Ford was the only president I covered who had the self-confidence to have a social drink in front of reporters, and occasionally, he would wander back to the press compartment at the rear of the plane, martini in hand, with no other purpose than to shoot the breeze. "Off the record, guys," he would announce, then he would spend a half hour or so joking and trading gossip.

Jimmy Carter seldom visited the press cabin, but we always kept an eye out for his daughter, Amy. Reporters sat around a table, and stewards usually placed a bowl of fruit and other snacks there. Amy loved to dash through the area and grab our fruit and candy. We always pretended to be angry, which seemed to delight her.

Carter had little use for the trappings of the modern presidency, and in the beginning of his presidency he would sometimes emerge from Air Force One carrying his own luggage, as he had done in the campaign, though he would soon abandon the practice. Of all the modern presidents, Carter probably had the unhappiest memories about the plane. He was on board the aircraft when aides called him in the early hours of election day 1980 and told him overnight polling showed he would not only lose to Ronald Reagan but lose badly. His top strategist, Hamilton Jordan, had stayed behind at the White House and told me it was one of the hardest calls that anyone on Carter's staff had ever made: "He was in Seattle when we reached him and he was flying on to Plains, Georgia, to vote, and our polling showed that he would not carry one state that he would be flying over. It was a tough night."

Ronald Reagan was the most fastidious of the modern presidents, and the first thing he would do upon boarding Air Force One was to change into comfortable clothing. He kept on his white shirt and tie, but always removed his coat and exchanged his trousers for a pair of sweat pants. It was an unusual sartorial combination — shirt and tie, polished wingtips, and sweat pants — but the Old Actor knew the place where fashion statements counted was not backstage but before the audience. Unlike Ford, Reagan seldom visited the section of the plane where reporters sat unless he had something specific he wanted to tell them, but the visits were always pleasant. Mrs. Reagan would usually accompany him and would hand out chocolates to the reporters.

No president enjoyed Air Force One more than Bill Clinton, who liked company as much as Richard Nixon liked being alone. For Clinton, Air Force One was the place for marathon conversations that would begin at some far-away capital and go on through the night, until the plane finally returned to Andrews.

Mark Knoller, the CBS News correspondent who has traveled hundreds of thousands of miles on Air Force One, remembers that on some long flights, Clinton would show up in the press cabin and talk for hours. "Sometimes you got the feeling that he started at the front of the plane and worked his way down the rows of passengers and once he wore them out, he would make his way to the press area and talk to us," Knoller said. "The man could really talk, but it was always interesting."

During the Clinton years, it was First Lady Hillary Rodham Clinton, not the president, who set the tone for everything on board, including the food. "If Mrs. Clinton was with us, the menu leaned heavily to chicken Caesar salads with low-cal dressing," Knoller said. "If the president was traveling alone, you could usually get a good old-fashioned cheeseburger."

John Kennedy was the first president to ride aboard a plane called Air Force One, and each succeeding president has used the plane more than his predecessor. Clinton traveled more than any of them. In eight years, he visited nearly as many foreign countries as the combined total of the three presidents who preceded him.

As might be expected, Air Force One is equipped with the most sophisticated and highly classified communications and defensive systems available, but the plane's pilots and crews have often found themselves relying on unconventional methods to meet the demands of presidents and resolve the problems that have occurred over the years.

Crewmen during Lyndon Johnson's presidency remember that he wanted a separate air-conditioning unit to control the temperature in his private compartment. When that proved impossible, engineers installed a switch marked "hotter-cooler" next to Johnson's chair. The switch was not connected to the aircraft's cooling system, but when Johnson adjusted it, a light flashed on the flight engineer's console and the engineer adjusted the temperature accordingly. Johnson never knew the switch was a phony and pronounced the new system "just fine."

Schieffer interviews President Clinton at the White House for *Face the Nation* in 1995. One of the longest-running news programs in television history, *Face the Nation* premiered on CBS on November 7, 1954. The chief Washington correspondent for CBS News, Schieffer has anchored the program since 1991.

In a more serious situation, in the minutes after the September 11 attacks when President George W. Bush broke off a public appearance in Florida and was rushed aboard Air Force One for safety, the crew again resorted to unconventional means. Fearing terrorists might try to target the plane by homing in on their radio transmissions, the pilots turned off all communications gear and used their personal cell phones to talk to Federal Aviation Officials and ground controllers.

Famous airplanes — the Wright Flyers, the *Spirit of St. Louis*, and the *Enola Gay* — have long been a part of the American story. But no plane has ever been remembered in the way we have come to regard Air Force One. Like the Washington Monument and the other symbols of America that we have come to know so well, it evokes our history. In this book, Von Hardesty takes us on board this unique set of planes and gives us a great ride. More than just the history of an airplane, it is a flight into the past and the events large and small that have shaped us as a nation.

The Loftiest Chariot

IN THE SUMMER of 1986, the Boeing plant in Everett, Washington, became the cocoon for a dramatic transformation of Air Force One. Boeing engineers were busy with the construction of two wide-body 747-200B airliners for White House service. These presidential jets, if slightly behind schedule and very costly, represented a quantum leap in size, range, and elegant appointments. The new jumbo jets dwarfed an earlier generation of venerable Boeing 707s that had flown American presidents for a quarter century.

Hugh Sidey, *Time* magazine's veteran White House reporter, alerted the public to these extraordinary aircraft. In his article "The Loftiest Chariot," Sidey quoted the ancient historian Ammianus Marcellinus, who once had observed that high-ranking nobles in the final days of the Roman Empire "measure[d] their rank and consequence according to the loftiness of their chariots." And, Sidey ruefully observed, "If old Marcellinus were around today he might be fretting about the future of the U.S., because we are about to put the President in the loftiest chariot that man has yet devised."[1]

Sidey's arcane reference to Marcellinus was a provoca-

Opposite: On his way to Grand Rapids, Michigan, President George W. Bush enters Air Force One on February 29, 2001. En route, he called Ariel Sharon to congratulate him on being elected Israel's prime minister. *Above:* A view of the current Air Force One, a Boeing 747-200B. Two Boeing 747s are attached to the 89th Airlift Wing at Andrews Air Force Base to serve as the primary aircraft for White House air travel operations.

tive way to suggest that heads of state throughout history often required special conveyances. In the time of Marcellinus, during the fourth century A.D., chariots still served in war, raced in the hippodromes, and offered the political elite a convenient way to showcase their status. The most splendid Roman chariots were the *quadrigae,* which were pulled by four horses. Roman emperors decorated their chariots in gold, wreaths, and elaborate ornamentation. The imperial chariot — often pulled by four white horses — was elevated, so the emperor stood above the crowd and became the most conspicuous personage in any triumphal procession. In Rome, the chariot was a symbol of power and ostentation, a distant analog for Air Force One.

When President George H. W. Bush finally took custody of the first 747-200B in 1990, there was no small amount of public debate on the perceived regal trappings that were now associated with presidential travel. Critics arose to describe the new Air Force One as a "flying palace" or an airborne "Taj Mahal." Air Force One, with its stunning blue, white, and silver livery, seemed to embody the worst fears of those concerned with the specter of an "Imperial Presidency."

Three American presidents on travel: (*top to bottom*) George H. W. Bush, Harry S. Truman, and Dwight D. Eisenhower. In these critical moments boarding and exiting the plane, all eyes are fixed on the president.

President Bush, however, defended the new Air Force One. He acknowledged that his aircraft indeed was "majestic" and "grand," but not necessarily an unseemly display of ostentation: "It's not fancy, with gold bathroom fittings and plush carpets. . . . No mirrors on the ceiling, no circular beds, no Jacuzzis, no bidets even. But man, oh man, is it comfortable."[2]

The actual design of Air Force One reveals its serious purpose, something quite separate from opulence and pretense. The interior décor is one of earth tones, with brown, rust, and pastel shades evoking a relaxed atmosphere, not unlike that of a modern hotel. The plane is divided into three levels: the lowest level houses cargo and special equipment; the middle level accommodates passengers and the forward presidential compartment; and the upper level is reserved for a high-tech communications center. The president's compartment consists of an office, a lounge, and a bathroom with shower. There he has access to state-of-the-art communications equipment and may establish immediate contact with the far-flung American military or, in a relaxed moment, call a friend on his mobile phone. For meetings, the president joins his staff in a large conference room, which also doubles as a dining room. For the senior staff accompanying the president, there is a separate office area with comfortable leather seats that can be converted into desks for work. The press travels in a rear compartment in more Spartan accommodations. A total of seventy passengers can fit comfortably inside Air Force One. The plane is, in effect, a flying Oval Office, an extension of the White House. The president can work there with the same efficiency as if he were in the Oval Office.

The use of the call sign "Air Force One" became standard practice in the mid-1950s. How the familiar presidential designation found its way into operational use is a matter of some conjecture, but the most probable story relates to a routine flight of President Dwight Eisen-hower's *Columbine II* from Washington, D.C., to Florida. According to this account, *Columbine II* (at the time known as Air Force 610) briefly became confused with an Eastern Airlines flight bearing the number 610. While both aircraft were on separate flight paths, the fact that they were aloft and in close proximity to one another prompted a measure of concern among Federal Aviation Administration officials and the Secret Service. The incident did not, in fact, cause any great difficulty for the presidential pilot, Colonel Bill Draper, or pose a real danger to the president. However, Draper wished to avoid any future misunderstanding, so he chose a new call sign, "Air Force One," for the presidential plane, a designation he felt would be ideal for the exclusive use of the White House. In time, the press learned of the new call sign and began using it as the all-purpose name for the president's plane. "Air Force One" quickly entered the popular lexicon.

Technically, any U.S. Air Force plane carrying the president of the United States becomes Air Force One. This logic holds sway on other official presidential flights. For example, the U.S. Marine helicopter that flies the president from the White House grounds to Andrews Air Force Base becomes "Marine One." Even small shuttle aircraft may be transformed into Air Force One when carrying the president.

Currently, there are two identical Boeing 747-200B aircraft in White House service, designated VC-25A with tail numbers 28000 and 29000. The twin 747s still carry the distinctive blue, white, and silver livery designed by Raymond Loewy for President John F. Kennedy's legendary Air Force One (a Boeing 707 with tail number 26000). Outwardly, these presidential aircraft mirror the silhouette of their sister jumbo jets in commercial service, but they possess a whole range of special design features. Tall as a six-story building, each presidential 747 weighs more than 800,000 pounds when fully loaded. Both airplanes are powered by four General Electric CF6-80C2B1 jet engines, each supplying 56,700 pounds of thrust. Air Force One typically cruises at 600 miles per hour. These extraordinary planes — in actuality military versions of the Boeing commercial design — come equipped for in-flight refueling, giving the president the option to remain aloft for an extended period in any emergency or even to circumnavigate the globe in a nonstop flight.

Given the heightened concern in the modern era for the personal security of the president, the design of Air Force One embodies the latest advances in avionics and defensive capabilities. While the exact nature of these systems remains highly classified, it is known that Air Force One possesses electronic counter-measures to jam enemy radar and to escape a missile attack. Even the elaborate wiring on the presidential 747s (over a million and a quarter feet of it, twice the amount of wiring on a standard jumbo jet) is shielded against the impact of an electromagnetic pulse — the wave of energy released in a nuclear explosion.

The twin presidential 747s, operated and maintained by the elite 89th Airlift Wing, are housed at a special maintenance and support facility at Andrews Air Force Base — a huge complex a few miles southeast of Washington, D.C., surrounded by guards, fences, and high-tech sensors to detect any unauthorized visitors. The hangar that houses the aircraft is brightly illuminated, spacious, and ultramodern, a fitting tribute to the high seriousness associated with presidential air travel. The mission of the 89th Airlift Wing is straightforward: to provide the president of the United States with a speedy and assured means of air travel to any domestic or foreign destination.

Highly skilled U.S. Air Force stewards provide a variety of services for the president and his guests. Among their many tasks, stewards anonymously buy food supplies of the highest quality and freshness for the airplane at local supermarkets — enough victuals for up to two thousand meals. Working in an area that occupies two full-size galleys, the steward crew can prepare up to one hundred meals at a sitting. The twenty-six-member crew who run Air Force One come to their prestigious assignment only after careful screening, and they reflect a wide variety of specializations. For example, a staff doctor oversees an elaborate medical facility with a fully stocked pharmacy, emergency-room equipment, and even a fold-out operating table. Contingency planning influences every aspect of Air Force One operations.

The fabled airplanes with the special designator "Air Force One" have been the set piece in more than one high drama in American history. Many who observed the role of Air Force One in the unfolding events of September 11, 2001, also remembered another episode involving a presidential airplane: President Kennedy and First Lady Jacqueline Kennedy's flight to Dallas, Texas, on November 22, 1963. Before the sun had set on that traumatic day, Kennedy would be assassinated and Air Force One transformed into a hearse for a long and mournful flight back to Washington.

Presidential aircraft have been center stage in numerous crises in American history, flying chief executives into war zones and to international summits and on myriad domestic trips to link the White House with the nation. By the end of the twentieth century, Air Force One had evolved into an essential arm of the American presidency, serving as an international symbol of the United States of America. With the advent of this remarkable high-tech flying machine, the peripatetic style of modern presidents became commonplace.

Presidential air travel often includes the first lady, as shown in these images: (*top to bottom*) John F. Kennedy and Jacqueline Kennedy; Lyndon B. Johnson and Lady Bird Johnson; and Ronald W. Reagan and Nancy Reagan.

"There are two places where the [president's] illumination shines the most. The first is the White House itself. The second is Air Force One." Jack Valenti, White House special assistant

Storm clouds gather over Air Force One on a tarmac in Paris, France. The modern Boeing 747-200B jumbo jet adds a new level of comfort and technical sophistication to presidential air travel, offering an American president unparalleled global reach.

Chapter One Pathways to Air Force One

THE MODERN INCARNATION of Air Force One — a 747-200B equipped with the latest high-tech communications and capable of flying 7,800 miles nonstop — stands in sharp contrast to earlier modes of travel for American presidents. Before the twentieth century, people — even presidents — moved about a vast continent in a variety of ways: on horseback; in coaches, wagons, and shays; on slow-moving, smoky trains; and on rafts, barges, steamboats, or ships.

America was an agrarian country, with the bulk of its population dispersed across an enormous expanse on farms and in small towns. The horse enjoyed a central role in the scheme of things. For certain, travel had acquired new efficiency with the building of canals and railroads, but boats and trains followed fixed routes and timetables. Overland travel still required the horse for the individual rider or to pull coaches or buggies.

Travel was never easy. Most pre-modern "highways" were primitive at best, lacking permanent roadbeds and subject to the ravages of weather. Taking the stage for a 1,200-mile journey from Boston to Savannah in the early nineteenth century required at minimum twenty-two days, assuming the traveler could maintain the extraordinary pace of more than fifty miles per day. Travel in the spring

Opposite: **President Washington, mounted on a white horse, arrives in New York on November 25, 1783, and is greeted enthusiastically by his countrymen.**
Above: **President Jackson arrives at the White House in 1829 for his inauguration after an arduous overland journey by riverboat and carriage from Tennessee.**

or fall often was slowed, or even stopped, by sudden rains, which could transform the primitive artery into an impassable river of mud.

The Founding Fathers

From the time of the Revolutionary War to the early years of the Republic, the Founding Fathers had to contend with the adversities associated with travel. Even with the swiftest and most comfortable horse-drawn carriage, they knew firsthand the enormous restraints of time and distance the conditions of American roads imposed on any traveler. Furthermore, there were additional problems when one reached a river or body of water: ferries often operated on irregular schedules, and severe snow and ice in winter posed problems for anyone seeking passage to a distant shore.

George Washington had been a land surveyor and a soldier in colonial America, a man who had traveled widely, even to remote locales on the American frontier. As president, he traveled frequently from his home in northern Virginia to New York and Philadelphia, a necessity in those formative days of the United States before the new capital was established in Washington, D.C. Wherever America's first president traveled, he drew crowds and sparked popular interest in his itinerary, adding special ambience to any inn or home that could make the genuine claim "Washington slept here."

Washington's successor, John Adams, was also a seasoned traveler. He was often on the road during the Revolutionary War, braving the cruel New England winters and enduring the rigors of colonial roads to attend sessions of the Continental Congress. Adams took great delight in the colonial inns. He was a man who loved "the food — wild goose on a spit, punch, wine, bread and cheese, apples — and a leisurely pipe afterward, while toasting himself at the fire."[1] Adams's sojourns at such inns also offered lively conversation and the sharing of news, where, in his words, the "scenes and characters" were worthy of "the amusement of a Swift or even a Shakespeare."[2]

Thomas Jefferson and James Madison set the standard for presidential travel in the early part of the nineteenth century. Members of Virginia's landed gentry, they traveled infrequently during their tenures as president. Typically, they followed restricted itineraries from their estates in central Virginia to the new capital in Washington, either by horseback or carriage, often staying with friends along the way. They stayed in Washington for only part of the year and made few public appearances. From July to October, when Washington's heat and humidity became unbearable, they escaped to the relative comfort of their estates, tucked against the Blue Ridge Mountains near Charlottesville.

Travel for presidents — as for all Americans — was extremely arduous. The distance from Jefferson's estate to Washington was roughly 140 miles. The weather in that region is unpredictable, especially in the spring and fall. Jefferson often hired a free black, Davy Bowles, to accompany him. No elaborate security measures were deemed necessary in an age when few citizens interacted with the occupant of the White House.

On a good day of relentless travel, most often in a light carriage with a servant as escort, Jefferson averaged only twenty-five to thirty miles. He occasionally stayed at taverns along the way. Most taverns, in Jefferson's mind, were "tolerable" with decent folk in residence. But, unlike Adams, Jefferson rarely found inns in his native state to be an unalloyed pleasure on a long journey. Only brief stays at Madison's Montpelier estate and similar homes offered a suitably genteel setting for the president on his journeys to and from Washington.[3] While Jefferson read widely and took a keen interest in world affairs, he felt little if any wanderlust as president, being content within the familiar environs of Virginia and Washington.

Thomas Jefferson made a 140-mile overland trek from his estate at Monticello, near Charlottesville, Virginia, to Washington for his inauguration as president in 1801.

James Monroe and Andrew Jackson

The cloistered lifestyle of American presidents ended with the administration of James Monroe. Monroe's tenure as chief executive signaled a dramatic shift in the nature of presidential travel, one in which an American president broke out of the self-imposed boundaries of the White House to reach out to the public. He made two remarkable odysseys — one in 1817 and the other in 1819 — over a vast portion of the country, unwittingly paving the way for modern presidential travel.

On June 1, 1817, President Monroe departed Washington for an unforgettable tour of the northern states, a 2,000-mile journey that took the chief executive up the eastern seaboard to Portland, Maine (then a part of Massachusetts), and across New York and Lake Erie to Detroit in the Michigan territory. His motive was to inspect military installations in states and territories bordering British-controlled Canada. Americans retained vivid memories of the War of 1812, concluded just two years before, when the British had burned the Capitol and the White House. Monroe felt compelled to strengthen America's defenses to meet the challenge of any future war.

A man of great energy, Monroe was accustomed to the rigors of travel. He traveled simply and with dispatch, typically with his private secretary and one or two servants. For his trip to the northern states, Monroe moved across great stretches of the country without the trappings of a monarch: no advance team, no special armed escort, no fancy gold-embellished carriage with footmen, and no rehearsed pageantry. Congress had appropriated money only for a president's salary and official duties. There was no special fund for such an extraordinary trip, so Monroe drew on his own income, sold furniture, and even borrowed money from a bank.

The 1817 presidential journey brought Monroe into close proximity to the populace, giving his countrymen a rare opportunity to see their head of state. As newspapers began to chronicle the president's unannounced trip northward, huge crowds began to gather in cities to get a glimpse of him. Monroe had hoped to make his trip quietly and without fanfare, but he soon found himself overwhelmed by enthusiastic onlookers, as when an extraordinary crowd of forty thousand people packed the streets of Boston to see their country's leader. The remarkable journey displayed the powerful symbol of the president as a unifying figure for the young nation.

On March 30, 1819, President Monroe began a second tour, this time to the South, via steamship down the Potomac River to Norfolk, Virginia. His itinerary covered more

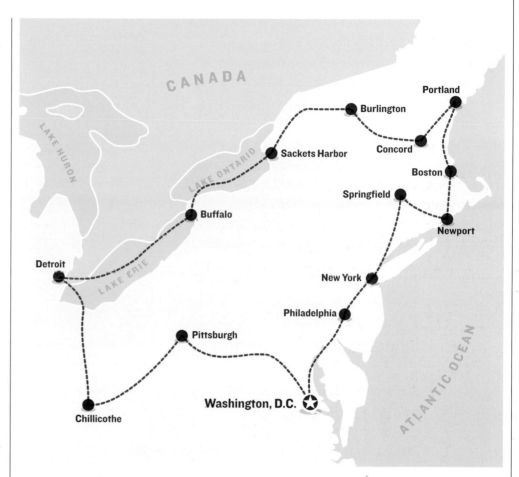

In 1817, James Monroe visited the northern states to inspect military fortifications. Monroe's unanticipated appearance in various cities — the first opportunity for the citizenry to see an American president in person — prompted considerable popular enthusiasm.

than 2,600 miles. Stops included Charleston, Savannah, and Nashville, among other towns, large and small. Monroe's journey followed a difficult passage through the hinterlands, as far north as Indiana, across Kentucky, and through the historic Cumberland Gap for the final leg home. He had hoped to visit the military installations under construction at Mobile Bay and New Orleans, but time and distance precluded adding these remote stops to the presidential itinerary. Monroe traveled with his two favorite nephews: Samuel Gouverneur and James Monroe Jr., a lieutenant serving in the army. As with his 1817 trip, the locals turned out in numbers to greet President Monroe with parades, speeches, militia escorts, and balls.

Monroe's many travels established a new dialogue between the president and the people. Many Americans took great pride in the fact that their leader moved about the country freely and encountered his fellow countrymen

Below: **President James Monroe made his second historic journey in 1819, this time to the southern states. Accompanied by a small entourage that included his two nephews, Monroe traveled through eight states, as far as Indiana on the Ohio River.**

with none of the pomp of a monarch. With time, of course, the simplicity of the Monroe trips would give way to more ornate rituals. Power — especially presidential power — evoked deference and the desire to provide lavish travel arrangements for any American president on the road. Wealthy Americans were quick to loan their elaborate carriages or finely appointed private train cars for presidential use. In the absence of an official government vehicle, more than one president made use of these loaned conveyances, justified as an expedient but the seedbed of much criticism.[4]

With this new precedent, Monroe's successors felt compelled to move regularly among the populace. When President-elect Andrew Jackson left his home in Tennessee to attend his inauguration in Washington, D.C., in January 1829, he followed the Cumberland and Ohio rivers northward to Pittsburgh, where he transferred to a stagecoach for an overland passage on the National Road to Washington. Jackson had asked for "no public shows or receptions," since only four weeks had passed since the death of his wife, Rachel. No declared period of mourning, however, dampened the widespread public enthusiasm for the new president. Wherever Jackson's stagecoach stopped to change horses or for rest, well-wishers rushed forward to shake hands with the newly elected president. Jackson dutifully met with his rustic followers throughout his journey, though some in his entourage found the "brutal familiarity" of the milling crowds a bit unnerving.[5] By this time, the notion that a president should travel and interact directly with his countrymen had been firmly established.

Abraham Lincoln
A generation later, on February 11, 1861, President-elect Abraham Lincoln left Springfield, Illinois, on a twelve-day trip to Washington for his inauguration. His train consisted of three cars for the 1,904-mile journey. Anticipating

Map labels:
ILLINOIS
INDIANA
OHIO
Washington, D.C.
Louisville
Corydon
Lexington
Charlottesville
VIRGINIA
KENTUCKY
Norfolk
Rogersville
N. CAROLINA
Nashville
TENNESSEE
Winchester
Huntsville
S. CAROLINA
Wilmington
MISSISSIPPI
ALABAMA
GEORGIA
Augusta
Charleston
Savannah

"Mr. Lincoln on the saddle looks about as ordinary in attire as the commonest man." Walt Whitman

Abraham Lincoln appears in front of his residence after his electoral campaign with Stephen Douglas. While railroads existed at the time, the mainstay for overland journeys was the horse or the horse-drawn carriage.

future presidential excursions, an additional car was later attached for journalists. Lincoln's route, by design, was long and circuitous: across Illinois, Indiana, and Ohio to Pittsburgh, Buffalo, Albany, New York City, Philadelphia, Harrisburg, and Baltimore. The final leg, from Baltimore to the District of Columbia, presented security risks, given the fact that many of the locals harbored deep resentment toward Lincoln and were in close proximity to the train route.

Lincoln's slow passage to Washington came at a time when the country was slipping into civil war. In fact, his election had been the occasion for the national crisis, one that in February 1861 seemed beyond compromise. In the weeks ahead, Lincoln faced open rebellion with the secession of South Carolina, which was soon followed by other southern states to form a new Confederate States of America. Once the die had been cast, the American Union entered into a bloody civil war lasting four years — a

conflict that, in the end, would claim in the assassination of Abraham Lincoln one of its last victims.

Special care was taken to provide a safe passage for Lincoln on his long rail journey to Washington. To prevent sabotage of the train, flagmen were stationed at every crossing and at half-mile intervals along the track. There was no official military guard for Lincoln, but several volunteer army officers, including a muscular bodyguard named Ward Hill Lamon, stood at the president-elect's side throughout the long trek to Washington.

Lincoln shared Andrew Jackson's notion that a national leader in a democratic society must retain close contact with the public. "It would never do," Lincoln once said, "for a president to have guards with drawn sabres at his door, as if he fancied he were trying to be, or assuming to be, an emperor."[6] Consequently, Lincoln possessed a certain bravado, or perhaps fatalism, about his safety. He passed through Baltimore in 1861 unscathed despite many rumors of an assassination plot. He traveled with minimal escort to various battlefields. And at the close of the war — just weeks before his assassination in Ford's Theater — Lincoln made a high-risk trek to occupied Richmond to visit the devastated capital of the Confederacy.

Walt Whitman has left us a portrait of Lincoln in wartime Washington that suggests security measures, if not complete or ultimately effectual, were nevertheless in place: "I see the President almost every day as I happen to live where he passes to or from his lodgings out of town. He never sleeps at the White House during the hot season, but has quarters at a healthy location some three miles north of the city, the Soldiers' home. . . . I saw him this morning about 8½ coming in to business, riding on Vermont Avenue, near L Street. He always has a company of twenty-five or thirty cavalry with sabers drawn and held upright over their shoulders. They say this guard was against his personal wish, but he let his counselors have their way."[7]

Top right: Lincoln receives an enthusiastic reception in Cleveland, Ohio, en route aboard his special train to his inauguration in Washington, D.C., in 1861.
Bottom right: The citizenry of Buffalo, New York, also have a rare occasion to see the new President-elect Lincoln.
Far right: Lincoln arrives at New York City's Hudson River depot to be greeted by a large crowd on the same journey to Washington.

Lincoln's apparent concession to war-induced security measures in a city with many Southern sympathizers, however, did not mean a complete abandonment of the informality that surrounded presidential travel in the nineteenth century. Despite the manifest dangers he did move about freely, sometimes with his wife in a carriage, on horseback, or alone in a carriage with his son riding as escort on his pony. Whitman remembered Lincoln on the streets of the capital: "Mr. Lincoln on the saddle generally rides a good-sized, easy-going grey horse, is dressed in plain black, somewhat rusty and dusty, wears a black stiff hat, and looks about as ordinary in attire . . . as the commonest man."[8]

For escort on these more impromptu excursions, the president enjoyed only a small company of guards, a lieutenant riding at his side, with several cavalrymen bringing up the rear. The slow trot of the cortege prompted little notice in the streets of Washington, even as the president entered Lafayette Square on his way to the White House.

However, whenever Lincoln traveled around the city in an open carriage, Whitman noticed that his escorts had their sabers drawn. Lincoln occasionally visited Secretary of War Edwin McMasters Stanton at his residence on K Street, where Stanton met the president's carriage in the street for an extended conversation.

Compared with modern standards, the modesty of the security for Lincoln appears reckless. But Lincoln lived in a society where the president was still considered a citizen leader, the first among equals, undeserving of special guards or the exalted status typical of European royalty. Even in the dangerous context of the Civil War, Lincoln himself accepted protection only reluctantly, telling Secretary Stanton on the eve of his risk-filled trip to Richmond, "I will take care of myself."[9]

Lincoln's assassination at Ford's Theater on April 14, 1865, did not significantly alter the easy-going style of presidential travel in subsequent decades. The later

"I have rather a strange objection to talking from the back platform of a train. I like a platform that stays put." Woodrow Wilson

assassinations of James Garfield (in 1879) and William McKinley (in 1901) bore testimony to the minimalist protection offered American presidents in the nineteenth century. In those days, the U.S. Secret Service was a division of the Treasury Department organized to combat counterfeiting. Only in the aftermath of the McKinley assassination did the Secret Service assume the responsibility of protecting the president of the United States.

New Modes of Presidential Travel

Presidential travel in the decades following the Civil War made full use of America's maturing railroad network. The establishment of a transcontinental railroad allowed Rutherford B. Hayes to become the first president to visit the West Coast, an important symbolic act of the American presidency. Hayes was referred to as "Rutherford the Rover" because of his many travels, renewing the tradition established by Monroe of bringing the presidency closer to the people.

The frequent use of trains by presidents in the nineteenth century and into the early decades of the twentieth century gave birth to renewed concern over the perceived monarchical aspects of the American presidency. Typically, presidents traveled in private cars, which often were richly appointed. By necessity, these train cars were borrowed from railway moguls and rich Americans, because no funds had ever been appropriated by Congress for the construction of special railway cars for the exclusive use of the chief executive. One private car, dubbed the "Maryland," served several presidents in grand style, including Rutherford B. Hayes, Grover Cleveland, Benjamin Harrison, and William McKinley. More a palace on rails, it was fifty-one feet long with four separate compartments. The parlor was lavish, with sofa, marble-top table, chairs, and decorative mirrors. Such luxury renewed the old debate on what is appropriate for presidential travel in a democracy.

Opposite: President Theodore Roosevelt (*center*) is shown with two unidentified men in front of a railway car, date unknown. Railroads provided the primary mode of transport for American presidents in the late nineteenth and early twentieth centuries.
Above: President Woodrow Wilson, accompanied by his wife Ellen, rides in an open convertible to his first inauguration. Wilson's immediate predecessor, William Taft, purchased the first official White House limousine.

Decades later, in the presidency of Franklin D. Roosevelt, the Secret Service fitted a special train car for presidential use. The "Ferdinand Magellan" was one of six built by the Pullman Company for rental by the federal government. The stress was on security, not luxury: the Magellan's steel-reinforced roof, bulletproof glass, and heavy armor plating gave President Roosevelt unparalleled security from gunfire or bombs. The Magellan also served President Harry S. Truman.[10]

At the turn of the twentieth century, the invention of the internal combustion engine signaled yet another mode of presidential travel — the automobile. The White House purchased the first presidential limousine, a seven-passenger White Model "M" touring car, during the administration of William Taft. Taft's successor, Woodrow Wilson, in turn acquired his own presidential vehicle, a Pierce-Arrow luxury sedan adorned with the presidential seal. These early limousines set a standard for luxury and comfort for successive administrations. Today, the automobile is a vital part of any president's ensemble of vehicles, essential for short-distance travel.[11]

Among all the technological marvels of the twentieth century, the airplane naturally attracted the greatest attention. Early flying machines, built of wood and fabric, were notoriously unsafe. Yet the airplane prompted widespread dreams of commercial airliners linking together the country, perhaps continents, in one vast network for travelers. In time, aviation technology would match human aspirations for swift and comfortable travel, with the airplane undergoing a dramatic evolution. World leaders, including American presidents, soon experimented with the airplane as the vehicle of choice to reach any destination in comfort and safety. The story of today's Air Force One begins with this great leap forward in presidential travel.

THE DAWN OF PRESIDENTIAL AIR TRAVEL may be traced to Kinloch Field near St. Louis, Missouri, on October 11, 1910. On that day, Theodore Roosevelt arrived at the dirt airstrip in a motorcade that included Herbert S. Hadley, the governor of Missouri, and several local dignitaries. The Roosevelt party had arrived at Kinloch to witness firsthand the technological marvel of the age — the airplane. Only seven years had elapsed since the Wright brothers had flown at Kitty Hawk, North Carolina. What happened at the Kinloch air show was fortuitously recorded on three and one half minutes of celluloid, preserved today in the Library of Congress.

The short film, capturing a rare moment at the dawn of the Air Age, shows Roosevelt taking a plane ride in a Wright Flyer, flown by Arch Hoxsey, an intrepid aviator who had just finished a record-making flight from Springfield, Illinois. History records that the celebrated plane ride was unscripted. The former chief executive — to the amazement and apprehension of his entourage — accepted the offer of a plane ride without hesitation. "You know I didn't intend to do it," Roosevelt later told a *New York Times* reporter, "but when I saw the thing there, I could not resist it."[1]

The former commander of the Rough Riders was no stranger to risk or adventure. In 1905, as U.S. president,

Opposite: Former president Theodore Roosevelt established an important milestone when he joined pilot Arch Hoxsey for a ride in a Wright Flyer on October II, 1910.
Above: Another image of Roosevelt seated in a Wright Flyer. The historic flight took place at Kinloch Field near St. Louis, Missouri, where the former president had arrived with the governor and local dignitaries to see an air show.

he had taken a dive in a submarine, arguably a more dangerous invention of that era. Again, at Kinloch, Americans learned that Theodore Roosevelt possessed the spirit of an adventurer.

One contemporary account of the plane ride suggested that Arch Hoxsey impulsively proposed the aerial jaunt by saying, "I want you to take a short spin with me in the air. You can, with perfect safety, trust yourself in my hands." Roosevelt replied, "Now?" Seeing that he had indeed sparked Roosevelt's interest, Hoxsey quickly responded: "Yes, this is as good a time as we can ever get. It is calm, and ideal flying machine weather. Will you go?" Boldly, Roosevelt walked to the Wright biplane, crawled through struts and strands of wires, and seated himself for the historic flight.[2]

The flight itself was a controlled affair. Given the fact his passenger was Theodore Roosevelt, Hoxsey did not wish to be responsible for any mishap or injury. Consequently, he never exceeded the altitude of 200 feet, and he steered his flying machine in such a way that he could land easily in the event of an emergency.

During the flight Roosevelt enjoyed himself immensely, waving his hat to the cheering crowd below. As a celebrity passenger, he had given the still fledgling aviation world a welcome endorsement. And, in retrospect, Roosevelt —

even as a former president at the time — had set a powerful precedent with his personal identification with the new technology of flight.

Franklin Delano Roosevelt

Franklin Delano Roosevelt set the next milestone. In July 1932, Roosevelt, then governor of New York, flew to Chicago to accept the Democratic Party's nomination for president. Roosevelt reasoned that a flight to Chicago would add great drama to his electoral campaign. Airplanes were still considered unsafe by most Americans, despite Charles Lindbergh's campaign to promote commercial airlines as the most efficient mode of travel.

Public apprehensions, however, grew out of the real dangers associated with flying, including lingering memories of the recent death of Knute Rockne, the famed Notre Dame football coach, in an airplane crash on March 31, 1931. While en route from Kansas City to Los Angeles, his tri-motor plane had crashed in the Kansas farmlands. There were no survivors, and Rockne was dead at the age of forty-three. In this environment, Roosevelt's long-distance flight appeared foolhardy in the extreme to many Americans.

Franklin Roosevelt flew out of Albany's airport in a Ford Tri-Motor on the morning of July 1 in what proved to be a long, noisy, and uneventful passage to Chicago. FDR took a large entourage with him that included James A. Farley Jr., his campaign manager, his wife, and four of his children, Anna, James, Franklin Jr., and John. The flight to Chicago called for three scheduled stops. While en route, the newly nominated presidential candidate found time on the cramped airliner to work on his acceptance speech, as the other passengers enjoyed the view along the flight path. After landing at Chicago, Roosevelt was escorted by Mayor Anton Cermak in a motorcade to the Democratic convention, where the triumphal nominee

Opposite: **Franklin Delano Roosevelt flies from Albany, New York, for Chicago on July 1, 1932, to accept the Democratic Party's nomination for president. Pictured with FDR (*center to right*) are his son Elliot, wife Eleanor, and son John.**
Above: **FDR flew to Chicago in a Ford Tri-Motor airplane, at the time a widely used airliner for long-distance air travel. The cross-country aerial trek required three stops.**

received a tumultuous response. No presidential nominee had ever assumed the mantle of leadership in such a dramatic fashion, descending from the heavens in an airplane, the technical marvel of the twentieth century.

More than a decade would pass before Roosevelt flew again. FDR still preferred the train, in particular his fabled private rail car, the "Ferdinand Magellan." White House correspondent Merriman Smith remembered that in those days presidential travel reflected a chief executive's personality and style, even his idiosyncrasies. "One simple reason," Smith wrote, "is time. Trips took longer in those days. . . . Travel with FDR was, even in the context of the 1940s, amazingly leisurely. Mr. Roosevelt delighted in a slow-speed train. He knew the various roadbeds of the country better than some railroad men. And he knew that reducing the rate of speed meant an easier ride. He also wanted the opportunity to sit by the window

Below: FDR, then governor of New York, boards a Pennsylvania Railroad car for a trip to Warm Springs, Georgia, in November 1931. *Bottom:* As president, Franklin Roosevelt made extensive use of a rail car dubbed the "Ferdinand Magellan."

of his private car and study the passing countryside."[3]

The president's demand for a deliberate pace often meant a forward speed of just thirty-five miles per hour, not even sufficient to recharge the batteries on the sleeping cars. For the reporters on board, the slow-moving presidential train often led to considerable boredom, once prompting Smith to ride atop the engine cab for a long stretch across Oklahoma for some excitement.

In time, such a genteel style of travel became problematic for Roosevelt, as the scope and demands of his office required a more efficient and secure means to reach a destination. And, in the context of World War II, Roosevelt found the airplane to be indispensable for his travel to distant parts of the globe.

As early as the mid-1930s some planners apparently discussed using Curtiss YC-30 Condor airplanes for presidential use, although this option never took any concrete form. In 1935 a small number of these obsolete biplanes were stationed at Bolling Field near Washington, but they

were never mobilized for White House service. Also, the U.S. Navy operated a Douglas Dolphin RD-2 seaplane for flights out of the Potomac River, an aircraft regarded by many as ideal for presidential use. But the Dolphin never was used by FDR, although the seaplane flew mail and guests to the White House.[4]

One odd aircraft, a transport version of the Consolidated B-24D Liberator bomber (military designation C-87), did find its way into White House service during World War II, but not as a presidential aircraft. Called *Guess Where II*, the modified C-87 was attached to the White House in 1943–44 as part of the 503rd Army Air Base Unit, or "Brass Hat Squadron," stationed at Washington's National Airport. The *Guess Where II* carried a special C-54 fuel tank for added range. The interior consisted of several compartments, not unlike a Pullman train car, supplemented with a galley and two lavatories. The plane could accommodate twenty people on day flights and berths for nine to sleep in some measure of comfort on

PULLMAN

FERDINAND MAGELLAN

U.S. Nº 1

"I said a little prayer that our plane would land us safely in Belém and not come down in the jungle." Eleanor Roosevelt

night flights. From the outside, the *Guess Where II* appeared like any other military transport parked at National Airport, except for the fact that a special guard force surrounded it at all times. Though never pressed into presidential duty, in 1944 the plane flew First Lady Eleanor Roosevelt on a 13,000-mile flight to the Caribbean and South America to inspect military bases.

As World War II unfolded, President Roosevelt found it necessary to attend three major wartime conferences with Allied leaders: Casablanca in North Africa in January 1943; Tehran, Iran, in November 1943; and, finally, Yalta in the Crimea in February 1945. These pivotal conferences shaped the course of the war and, in the case of Yalta, drew up the post-war diplomatic settlement for Europe and Asia. Travel to these distant points required the systematic use of aircraft, in a context of high secrecy and careful planning to provide security for the president.

Roosevelt's first trip abroad to attend the ten-day Casablanca conference with British prime minister

Winston Churchill and leader of the Free French Charles de Gaulle called for an unprecedented flight across the Atlantic Ocean. The decision to fly over the Atlantic, as opposed to crossing by boat, reflected the fact that German submarines still posed a formidable threat. Even after landing at Casablanca, there were security concerns. The city, nominally under Allied control, was known to harbor Nazi spies and French collaborators with the Axis powers. At the time, Berlin had actually intercepted a coded Allied message that spoke of an upcoming summit. But German intelligence erroneously translated the word "Casablanca" to mean literally the "White House," suggesting the proposed conclave would be in Washington.[5]

Departing Washington by train at 10:30 P.M. on January 9, 1943, Roosevelt traveled southward in the Magellan, his private rail car. He was accompanied by his chief advisor, Harry Hopkins, and a select group of aides: Grace G. Tully, his personal secretary; Captain John L. McCrea, the White House physician; Admiral William D.

Below: Eleanor Roosevelt, as FDR's special representative, flew on a modified B-24 Liberator bomber (C-87A), the *Guess Where II*.
Bottom: Eleanor Roosevelt with her official party next to *Guess Where II* in Brazil, March 1944.

"He acted like a sixteen-year-old...happy and interested."

Harry Hopkins, special assistant to FDR

that a "Mr. Jones" was "Passenger No. One," to be accompanied by a small entourage of fellow travelers, including Hopkins, Leahy, and six other men. In time, Cone learned that this indeed was a presidential party.

Hopkins later recalled that his boss approached the trip to Casablanca with keen interest and no small amount of emotion: "I sat with him, strapped in, as the plane rose from the water — and he acted like a sixteen-year-old, for he has done no flying since he was president. The trip was smooth, the president was happy and interested."[6]

An escort of thirty-six fighters flew as protective cover for the *Dixie Clipper*. Flying at an altitude of nine thousand feet, the president and his party enjoyed breakfast on the flying boat. With the assistance of his valet, Arthur Prettyman, FDR changed into casual wear for the long flight: an open-collared shirt, sweater, and slacks. Always an attentive traveler, Roosevelt asked Captain Cone if they could fly over Henri Christophe's old Citadel near Haiti, a historic landmark he had visited years before as assistant secretary of the navy. Cone dutifully vectored the lumbering Boeing 314 over the citadel and then resumed his normal heading for Trinidad.

Staying overnight at Trinidad's Cocorite Airport, the presidential party resumed its journey the next day toward Belém, Brazil. FDR passed the hours in conversation, playing solitaire, and taking in the sights as the large plane cruised over the vast jungle terrain stretching to the horizon. Following the existing Pan Am Airways South Atlantic route, they reached Belém, where the president briefly toured the American military installations at the Brazilian coastal town before an evening departure for Africa.

The riskiest leg of the trip followed as the presidential air flotilla headed out over the South Atlantic. The night flight encountered turbulent air while en route, forcing Captain Cone to alter his altitude several times. FDR slept

Leahy; and other advisors specifically chosen for the delegation. A nervous Secret Service detachment accompanied the presidential party throughout the 16,965-mile journey to Morocco for the historic wartime conference.

The presidential party reached Miami, Florida, on January 11. Roosevelt was transported by car to nearby Dinner Key, the base for Pan Am Clipper flights. Here the president boarded a Boeing 314 flying boat, the *Dixie Clipper* (NC-05), for the long flight across the Atlantic. Moored nearby was a second seaplane, the *Atlantic Clipper* (NC-04), to be employed as a backup if needed. The Pan Am aircraft and crews had been mobilized during the war and placed under the command of the U.S. Navy.

At the controls of the *Dixie Clipper* was Captain Howard Cone, part of a crew of ten for the presidential flight. Before the journey, Cone merely had been told to be ready for a flight on January 11 with "priority one" passengers. When he examined the passenger manifest, it read

Opposite: **FDR flew clandestinely to North Africa to attend the Casablanca conference in January 1943. For the transatlantic trip, Roosevelt flew on Pan Am's Boeing 314 seaplane, the *Dixie Clipper*.** *Above:* **On board the *Dixie Clipper* during the 1943 flight, FDR confers with U.S. Navy captain Bryan Mau, who coordinated the unprecedented presidential flight to North Africa.**

FDR and the Pan Am Clipper

Clandestine Journey Launches a New Era in Presidential Travel

Hollywood took notice of Juan Trippe's Pan American Airways in 1936 with the feature-length film *China Clipper,* starring Humphrey Bogart. Popular fascination with Trippe's fabled flying boats traversing the Pacific Ocean had reached a new intensity by the late 1930s. Air travel on a Pan Am Clipper was fast compared to an ocean liner and rather expensive, not unlike a pricey ticket on the Concorde decades later.

Among all Pan Am's flying boats, the Boeing 314 was the ultimate, the high end of air travel in terms of power, luxury, and range. In 1936, Pan Am had ordered six of these huge four-engine flying planes with a range of 3,500 miles. Having earlier conquered the Pacific Ocean, Trippe now turned his eyes to the Atlantic. His goal was to sustain an ambitious schedule of transoceanic crossings on a global scale. Trippe assigned one of his new Boeing 314s, the *Yankee Clipper,* to inaugurate the world's first transatlantic service in May 1939, carrying a ton of mail from New York to Marseilles, France. A month later, another Pan Am flying boat, the *Dixie Clipper,* flew twenty-two well-heeled passengers across the North Atlantic — each paying $375 one-way and $675 for a round-trip, at the time astronomical ticket prices for air travel.[7]

The *Dixie Clipper,* of course, is best remembered for its place in the saga of presidential travel, having been chosen to fly President Franklin Roosevelt across the Atlantic in World War II for a conference in Morocco. The January 1943 event was the first of a sequence of major wartime conferences between Roosevelt, Winston Churchill, and other Allied leaders.

This particular flight possessed great drama because it marked the first time a sitting president had flown in an airplane, let alone on a long-distance flight across the submarine-infested Atlantic Ocean. The historic journey took place under great secrecy and involved considerable planning. The Pan Am Clippers, along with their flight crews, had been mobilized for the war effort. The *Dixie Clipper* offered the occupant of the White House a swift mode of transport to

Below: The *Dixie Clipper* in pre-war operations, shown here at the conclusion of a 1939 transatlantic flight from Port Washington, New York, to Lisbon, Portugal. *Right:* Pan Am Clippers flew a regular schedule from the United States to Europe and the Orient in the late 1930s. *Far right:* The flight deck on a Boeing 314 Pan Am Clipper. For the long-distance transoceanic flights, Pan Am required multiple crews.

bridge the Atlantic to reach distant Casablanca.

Roosevelt departed on the *Dixie Clipper* from Dinner Key Seaplane Base in Miami on January 11. Captain Howard M. Cone occupied the left seat of the Clipper, the senior member of a select group of

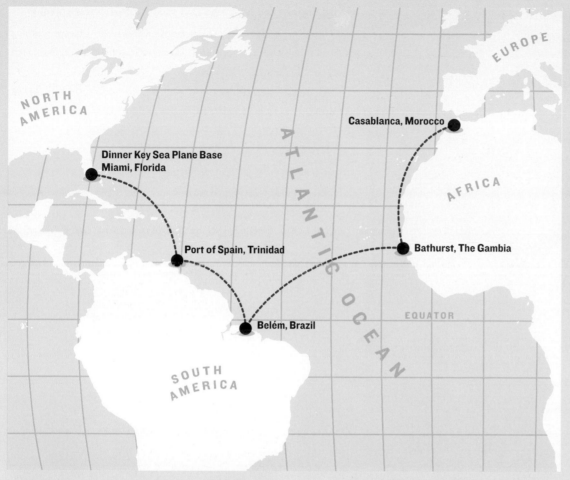

Dinner Key Sea Plane Base
Miami, Florida

Casablanca, Morocco

NORTH
AMERICA

EUROPE

AFRICA

ATLANTIC OCEAN

Port of Spain, Trinidad

Bathurst, The Gambia

Belém, Brazil

EQUATOR

SOUTH
AMERICA

return to Bathurst after the conference, Roosevelt boarded the *Dixie Clipper* for the return flight home.

For its time, the Boeing 314 indeed was a luxurious transoceanic airliner. The aircraft's fuselage section measured 109 feet; it was divided into two levels connected by a spiral staircase. Four Wright Double Cyclone engines, each rated at 1,500 horsepower, were required to lift the huge flying boat into the air and sustain it on long transoceanic flights. The spacious appointments of the *Dixie Clipper* allowed the partially paralyzed president to have his own stateroom, only slightly modified to accommodate its VIP passenger: a double bed had been installed to offer FDR some measure of comfort on the long-distance flight. And the trip took on a relaxed atmosphere, in which the president decided to dress in casual clothes. This same mood was apparent on the flight home, when the passengers and crew of the *Dixie Clipper* celebrated FDR's birthday with a special cake prepared for the event.

The *Dixie Clipper* in most respects mirrored the design and appointments of a typical Pan Am transoceanic airliner. Below the upper level, which housed the luggage compartment and cockpit, was a long fuselage section that included a labyrinth of walkways, galleys, dressing rooms, a dining room/lounge, seating for passengers, and even a crew's day cabin. Before the war, each Pan Am Boeing 314 Clipper included a deluxe cabin in the rear section that often served as a bridal suite.

The flight on the *Dixie Clipper* represented an important milestone in presidential air travel, getting the president to his appointed rounds with a unique blend of speed and luxury.

personnel chosen to fly the president to North Africa. Eight passengers accompanied the president. The trip unfolded in three segments: the first leg, covering more than 1,600 miles, took the president to Port of Spain, Trinidad, on the first day; then a flight to Belém in Brazil covered another 1,200 miles in eight hours; and the final leg, the most tension-filled, saw the *Dixie Clipper* transport the president across 2,500 miles of ocean to Bathurst (today Banjul), the capital of British-controlled Gambia. From Bathurst, FDR flew on a C-54 passenger plane to Casablanca. Upon his

"This generation of Americans has a rendezvous with destiny." Franklin D. Roosevelt

President Franklin Roosevelt (*at right*) with members of his official party on board the *Dixie Clipper* during the 1943 flight to North Africa. Admiral W. D. Leahy is seated to the left of the president.

during most of the nineteen-hour crossing, while others in his official party moved about in pajamas and robes, taking in the relaxed atmosphere of the flying boat. Upon reaching the African coast at Bathurst, British Gambia, the presidential party transferred to a nearby airfield, where three camouflaged C-54 transports flew them to Casablanca.[8]

Winston Churchill's passage to Casablanca proved to be less pleasant. Flying from England in an American-made B-24 Liberator, the prime minister spent the hours en route in an unheated bomber, forced to sleep on a mattress in the rear of the fuselage. Lord Moran, his assistant, similarly situated that night, awakened with the noise of Churchill crawling away from his mattress, where he had burned his toe on the hot electrical connections of its heating device. Churchill spent the night trying to keep warm.

Lord Moran noted: "The PM is at a disadvantage in this kind of travel since he never wears anything at night but a silk vest. On his hands and knees, he cut a quaint figure with his big, bare, white bottom."[9]

At Casablanca, Roosevelt was joined by General Dwight D. Eisenhower and General George S. Patton, among other top-ranking American military, for the conference. The historic conclave was held at the Anfa Hotel, which was tightly secured with numerous anti-aircraft batteries and armed guards. Churchill and Roosevelt were housed in villas just fifty yards apart from one another. One critical result of the conference was the acquiescence of FDR to Churchill's plan for the invasion of Italy — the first step toward liberating Europe from Nazi occupation. At the time of the conference the battle of Stalingrad was still underway, a reminder that even as late as 1943 the Russians were still bearing the brunt of the land war. Joseph Stalin would not let his Allies forget this fact in the conferences ahead in Tehran and Yalta.

President Roosevelt's return to the United States followed roughly the old itinerary, with one major exception. After the C-54 transport flew him back to the Gambia, the president took a one-day side trip to Liberia. He then boarded the *Dixie Clipper* for the transatlantic flight home. The long excursion westward included a birthday party for the president on the flying boat. The *Dixie Clipper* reached Biscayne Bay on the afternoon of January 31, ending one of the more memorable presidential trips in history, the first overseas flights by a sitting president.

Michael Reilly, the Secret Service agent who accompanied Roosevelt on his overseas trips, observed that his boss was not necessarily a lover of airplanes. In Reilly's view, FDR embraced flying because of the speed it afforded him on high-priority missions across continents and oceans. "Rough weather aloft," Reilly remembered, was particularly hard on the partially paralyzed chief executive

"because he could never brace himself against the bumps and jolts with his legs as we could. And, although he never spoke of it, he must have realized that he had no chance of crawling away from a plane wreck."[10]

For the next stage in wartime diplomacy, Roosevelt traveled to Cairo and Tehran between November 11 and December 17, 1943. Given the great distances, it was

FDR cuts his birthday cake, prepared by the crew of the *Dixie Clipper,* on the return leg of the 1943 transatlantic trip. Presidential adviser Harry Hopkins is seated directly across the table from the president.

decided that FDR would travel on the USS *Iowa* on the transatlantic crossings to Morocco. Once he reached landfall in North Africa, he flew on a c-54 military transport to Cairo and Tehran. Major Otis F. Bryan served as his pilot. The conference at Tehran, in particular, was important, offering the occasion for the three Allied leaders — Roosevelt, Churchill, and Stalin — to meet. The trip offered some interludes for tourism for the American president. He visited ancient Carthage and flew along the Nile River to see the Egyptian pyramids. On his second overseas journey Roosevelt had traveled by land, sea, and air, covering a total 17,442 miles.[11]

The evolving scope of FDR's wartime travels set the stage for the designation of the first official presidential aircraft, a C-54 Skymaster transport known as "Project 51" but dubbed the *Sacred Cow* by the Washington press corps. In June 1944, the Douglas Aircraft plant in Santa Monica, California, delivered the air transport to the 503rd Army Air Base unit at Washington's National Airport (the predecessor of the 89th Airlift Wing currently responsible for Air Force One). Major Henry T. Myers served as pilot for the new presidential airplane. Joining Major Myers were a co-pilot and a crew of five men. The *Sacred Cow* boasted a capacity for fifteen passengers for day operations, with the facility for sleeping six on night flights, and at the time represented a quantum leap in technology. For the first time in the history of the White House, a president had at his disposal a special aircraft.

The new presidential aircraft reflected in its design the special needs of President Roosevelt: a battery-powered elevator, located in the rear section of the plane, allowed for easy access to and from the tarmac. For the polio-stricken Roosevelt, the elevator meant he would not have to use the cumbersome ramps to gain access to the plane. A collapsible steel wheelchair fit easily into the elevator, and once he was in the fuselage section of the plane, he could move freely down the aisle — even to the cockpit area, where he often seated himself in flight for observation and conversations with the pilot and co-pilot.

FDR's private compartment was fitted with a swivel chair, always in easy reach of an oxygen mask, a reading light, and a telephone connected to the cockpit and the three other staterooms adjoining the presidential suite.

Above: An interior view of President Franklin Roosevelt's plane, the *Sacred Cow*, shows his seat and communications center.
Right: The first military transport officially assigned for presidential service was the Douglas VC-54C *Sacred Cow*. During the president's trip to Yalta, the plane's serial number, 42-107451, was changed to 42-72252 "to confuse the enemy." The *Sacred Cow*, bearing its false serial number, is currently on display at the U.S. Air Force Museum in Dayton, Ohio.

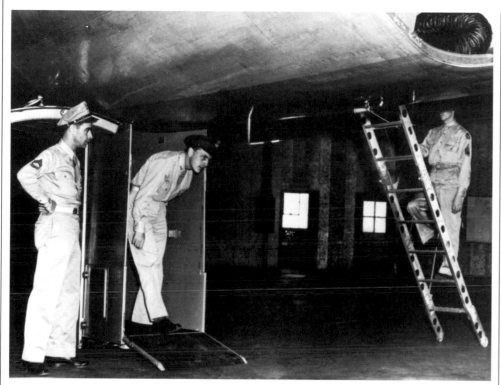

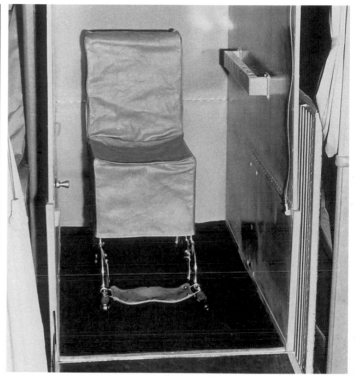

A large conference table, fitted on one side with maps, offered a place for meetings and casual conversation. Four instruments were mounted above the maps to allow the president to monitor the course of any flight: an air speed indicator, an altimeter, a compass, and a clock. Other interior appointments rounded out the design of the *Sacred Cow*: electric folding chairs, a galley, and a lavatory. For FDR, the presidential plane replicated the ambience of a Pullman car.[12]

The *Sacred Cow* became an important component in FDR's travel itinerary for his third and final wartime conference, at Yalta in February 1945. The purpose of the meeting between Roosevelt, Churchill, and Stalin was to review the current state of the war and, more importantly, to achieve an understanding on the map of the post-war world. With Stalin's armies occupying much of Eastern Europe and on the threshold of capturing Berlin, there was

Opposite: Another interior view of the *Sacred Cow*, shows the sofa, chair, and wall hangings. This presidential aircraft offered a real measure of comfort and luxury for long-distance trips.
Above, left: Crew members of the *Sacred Cow* inspect the elevator and access doors of the presidential plane in 1945.
Right: A special feature in the design of the *Sacred Cow* was an elevator, which allowed the wheelchair-bound FDR to enter and exit the plane with relative ease.

a thinly veiled threat to extend the communist empire into the heart of Europe. In return for Stalin's assistance in defeating Japan, there were further pressures to make concessions and a series of accommodations. The Yalta agreements would remain controversial: for some, they represented a necessary course of action for the Allies; for others, a series of ill-fated compromises that, in the end, would lead to another long-term conflict, the Cold War.

The Yalta conference itself was a dramatic affair, a pivotal moment in the course of World War II, set in the splendid Livadia Palace along the coast of the Black Sea, once a summer home for the tsars. Getting to Livadia, located outside Yalta on the Crimean Black Sea coast, was no easy task, especially for FDR, who was in poor health and lacked the stamina for a long trip by sea and air to the distant Crimea. President Roosevelt and his party boarded the USS *Quincy* on January 23, 1945, for the transatlantic crossing, reaching Malta on February 3. They then flew in the *Sacred Cow* from Malta to the Crimea as part of a huge delegation of seven hundred British and Americans, brought to the conference in twenty transports.

In preparation for the presidential flight to Yalta, Henry Myers (now a lieutenant colonel) and the crew of the *Sacred Cow* made a dry run to the Crimea to plot out the route and familiarize themselves with the protocols of flying into Soviet air space. While completing another dry run to Cairo, in anticipation of the president's return journey from Yalta, the *Sacred Cow* lost its second engine, forcing a hurried effort to substitute a new engine cannibalized from another C-54. The tradition of giving the presidential

airplane the highest priority in service and maintenance had been established with the *Sacred Cow*.[13]

Five P-38 fighters escorted the presidential airplane. Once FDR arrived at the Soviet airfield at Saki, he transferred to a car for a drive of eighty miles overland to Yalta. On February 12, he returned to Saki for another flight in the *Sacred Cow*, this time to Deservoir Field in Egypt. Later, the president again boarded the USS *Quincy* for the return voyage home.

Just two months later, on April 15, Americans received the stunning news that President Roosevelt had died at Warm Springs, Georgia. Having been elected to four terms as president, FDR had been a powerful leader in peace and war. However, he did not live to see the end of World War II or, for that matter, to contend with the issues raised in the wartime conferences, the forces that would shape the course of the Cold War in the decades after 1945.

Harry S. Truman

When Harry S. Truman assumed the American presidency in April 1945, he faced many daunting tasks, from presiding over the final prosecution of the war against Nazi Germany and Japan to dealing with the emerging Cold War with the Soviet Union in the aftermath the last Big Three conference at Potsdam, Germany, with Stalin. The Truman administration faced the menace of the Cold War in the post-war years. The president aggressively opposed any expansion of the communist bloc, as evident in his commitment of American forces to the Korean War, which broke out in the summer of 1950.

The growing utility — even necessity — of presidential aircraft soon became manifest to all. In time, too, these special airplanes increasingly became airborne symbols of American power and prestige. Always attentive to continuity on both major and minor issues, Truman became a regular passenger on the *Sacred Cow*, making extensive use of

President Harry S. Truman waves to the crowd as he departs Brussels for the Allied conference at Potsdam, Germany, on July 15, 1945. In the post-war world, American presidents would make increasing use of the airplane for travel.

The Presidential Airplane That Never Was

The Air Force Builds "The Dewdrop" for "President Dewey"

The presidential election of 1948 seemed a sure bet for the Republicans. Thomas E. Dewey of New York headed the ticket, with Governor Earl Warren of California as his running mate. Most pundits viewed President Harry S. Truman and his running mate, Alben Barkley, as destined for inevitable defeat. Truman's popularity had dropped precipitously in 1948, a reality that was mirrored in every poll.

Believing the polls, the U.S. Air Force decided to get ahead of the curve and prepare a new presidential plane for the predicted occupant of the White House. The Air Force had ten Lockheed Constellations on order at the time, and it seemed logical that one of these air transports could be config-

Left: First Lady Margaret Truman and President Truman stop for a photograph before boarding *The Dewdrop* on April 10, 1950.
Below: The *Dewdrop* crew of eight pose at Andrews Air Force Base in 1948.

ured for Tom Dewey. The goal was to have the Constellation ready in January 1949, the date everyone anticipated the Republican candidate would assume office as the president of the United States.

A large, sleek plane with a triple tail design, the Lockheed Constellation arguably was the most beautiful airliner of the pre-jet era. It featured a pressurized fuselage and was powered by four Wright R-3350 eighteen-cylinder radial engines, the most advanced piston engine of the time.

The special executive air force version of the Constellation (C-121) set aside for Dewey bore the designation VC-121B and was dubbed unofficially "The Dewdrop." Ironically, the plane was flown to Washington's National Airport on November 24, 1948, just days after the improbable victory of Harry Truman over Tom Dewey. Now reelected, President Truman found the whole affair amusing, and he refused to accept the Constellation as a replacement presidential plane, paraphrasing the lyrics from a popular song: "I don't want it — you can have it — it's too big for me!"

The ill-fated *Dewdrop* then entered a twilight existence as a backup VIP plane, often used by U.S. Air Force and cabinet officials. When flown by the secretary of the air force, it bore the official air force seal. During the Eisenhower years, the plane — now with the name *Dewdrop* on the nose — was used to transport Secretary of State John Foster Dulles. Under John F. Kennedy, the nickname was removed and the aircraft was mobilized as the primary plane for Secretary of the Air Force Donald Quarles. Thus ended one of the more bizarre episodes in the history of presidential airplanes.

"You have to remember it isn't for you. It's for the presidency." Harry S. Truman

the historic airplane for his own personal travel as well as loaning it to others for government-related trips. Truman left in place the elevator used by his predecessor, even using it on one occasion as a convenient means for his aged mother to board the aircraft for a family trip. The other interior appointments of the *Sacred Cow* were retained, including the sailing-ship pictures mounted on the fuselage walls by FDR. Only one upgrade came on Truman's orders: the installation of a thermometer to show the outside temperature.[14]

White House reporter Merriman Smith remembered the *Sacred Cow* during Truman's tenure in office as possessing "an unusually complete galley" equipped with "electric stove, refrigerator, food warmer, electric mixer, hot and cold water, toaster, food storage lockers, and a place

Below: The last flight of the *Sacred Cow,* with Major General Brooke Allen at the controls at Andrews Air Force Base on October 17, 1961. At the time of its retirement the presidential plane had flown over a million and a half miles.
Opposite: President Harry Truman exits the *Independence,* a C-118 military version of the DC-6 airliner, after a 1951 flight to Key West, Florida.

for storing ice cubes made by the refrigerator."[15] While the *Sacred Cow* possessed many creature comforts, when compared to modern presidential aircraft, it was a minimalist affair. For its time, though, the plane represented state-of-the-art air transport.

By 1946, the Truman administration welcomed the arrival of a new aircraft dedicated to White House use that would reflect a more modern design and the personality of the president. The U.S. Army Air Forces (later the independent U.S. Air Force) ordered a four-engine DC-6 airliner (C-118 military version) from Douglas Aircraft. The new White House airplane eventually received the name *Independence* (VC-118-DO). This name — the same as that of his hometown — fit well with President Truman, but there were other motives for its choice, in particular the concern that the Douglas airliner might otherwise acquire the nickname *Sacred Cow II.* Henry Myers again served briefly as the presidential pilot for the *Independence* and then left military service to become a commercial airline pilot. His replacement, Lieutenant Colonel Francis W. "Frenchie" Williams, had been the co-pilot on the *Independence*; his career also included a stint as a pilot for American Airlines.

The *Independence* represented the most modern piston-powered airliner in service at the time with its pressurized cabins and four 2,100-horsepower Pratt & Whitney engines (R-2800-34 Double Wasp CA-15 types). Its high-performance, advanced systems were apparent in other features: reversible pitch propellers, water injection added to the engines for increased thrust on takeoff, and radar mounted in the nose to detect heavy precipitation and storms up to thirty miles ahead.

The *Independence* cruised at around 315 miles per hour, and extra fuel tanks allowed for a range of 4,400 miles. The cockpit display mirrored the most advanced instrumentation then available: a radio altimeter, an electronic

A full view of VC-118-DO, the *Independence,* in flight, date and place unknown. The plane's distinctive blue and yellow livery, mimicking the head and feathers of an eagle, made a dramatic impact on presidential trips.

"It was a gaudy airplane, more likely to be mistaken for a flying circus than a 'Flying White House.'" Col. Ralph Albertazzie

The INDEPENDENCE

autopilot, advanced navigation instruments, and the latest radio communications gear. On board, the president had use of a radio teletype transmission system, allowing the chief executive to send and receive messages over a distance of 3,000 miles. The *Independence* marked a new level of technical sophistication in presidential aircraft.[16]

The *Independence* had been commissioned, appropriately, on July 4, 1947. Unlike the unadorned *Sacred Cow,* the new presidential airplane sported a stunning paint scheme in blue and yellow, portraying a stylized eagle's head and feathers extending from the nose back with three blue feathers sweeping up the vertical stabilizer. The nose, together with the cockpit windows, evoked an image of the eyes and beak of an eagle's head. The paint scheme was vivid and unforgettable. President Truman took great delight in the exotic livery of his new plane.[17]

Among all the flights of the *Independence,* Truman's long trek to Wake Island on October 15, 1950, was the most memorable. Here he met with General Douglas MacArthur, then military commander of United Nations forces in Korea, in a high-stakes conclave on the conduct of the war on the Korean peninsula. MacArthur had taken a forceful stand on the war, one that was often at odds with the more measured approach of the White House. The clash of wills became a defining moment for the Truman presidency. Ultimately, Truman decided to fire General MacArthur, stressing the importance of civilian control of war policy.

Dean Acheson's Excellent Adventures

Harry Truman Gives His Secretary of State the Ultimate Perk

For cabinet members, one of the most prized perks in Washington is the exclusive use of the presidential plane for official travel. Dean Acheson, Truman's secretary of state, pioneered the practice, and others, most notably Henry Kissinger, made it a tradition in the pursuit of high diplomacy. The use of a presidential aircraft became a subtle way to strengthen the hand of any official on a special mission for the White House: the plane projected the power and prestige of the American presidency.

Acheson often traveled on Truman's *Independence,* at his boss's insistence; for Acheson, it was "a most luxurious — for those days — DC-6 propeller plane." In 1949 he flew overnight on the *Independence* to Paris, where he met Andrei Vishinsky, the Soviet minister of foreign affairs. Vishinsky, the hardened prosecutor of Stalin's purges in the 1930s, stood in sharp contrast to the elegant, mustached Acheson. The Cold War conclave proved a success, and the presidential plane served as a speedy means to transport Acheson to and from Europe.

While Acheson's memories of the *Independence* were overwhelmingly affirmative, he experienced some white-knuckle flights. Later in 1949, accompanied by Kentucky senator John Sherman Cooper, he took a second diplomatic trip to Paris on the *Independence.* While landing in Canada to refuel, the party encountered foul weather. As Acheson recalled: "We ran into a thunderstorm during which a ball of fire seemed to pass through the President's cabin across the table where my wife and John sat facing me. John asked us casually whether this often happened. My wife, usually more truthful, answered, 'Quite.' Colonel Williams,

Harry Truman bids farewell to Secretary of State Dean Acheson and his wife on the eve of a trip to London and Paris in May 1950. Acheson made extensive use of the *Independence* for his diplomatic missions.

the skipper and pilot, told us that it required some later work on the sheathing of the plane but nothing to interfere with our journey."[18]

On December 20, 1950, on a return flight from Europe to Washington via the Azores, the plane made its departure in fog and freezing rain. Of all the takeoffs of the *Independence,* Acheson most vividly remembered this one: "At last, we got the signal and, heavily strapped in our seats, went

on a veritable buckboard ride down the runway. The liftoff brought blessed smoothness and, in minutes, bright sunshine above the five-hundred-foot fog."[19]

There were other memorable flights, as in 1952, when Acheson flew over the equator in the *Independence.* This occasion prompted a ruse by the pilot: "Suddenly," Acheson recalled, "he lifted the great ship in a surprising jump over the barrier and brought her safely over."[20]

Despite these unnerving experiences, the secretary of state in time acquired a strong bond with his favorite plane.

Many Americans considered MacArthur to be a war hero, and they viewed Truman's order as arbitrary and unjustified. In retrospect, the president's decision to call the meeting reflected both political and national security considerations of the White House. The hurriedly arranged meeting would not have been feasible without the existence of a presidential airplane with long-distance flight capabilities. The *Independence* flew the 7,000-mile journey to Wake Island in a remarkably short period of time.

In 1973, Merle Miller's oral biography of Truman, *Plain Speaking*, suggested a most bizarre incident involving the *Independence*: that the presidential airplane had been held in the traffic pattern over tiny Wake Island as a struggle ensued over whether the *Independence* or MacArthur's approaching plane should land first. The implication of the story was that the imperious General MacArthur had attempted to upstage President Truman by making a more dramatic landing after the president was on the ground. While the encounter on Wake Island possessed high drama and ultimately set the stage for MacArthur's firing, this particular incident did not in fact take place. The *Independence* made a normal landing on the airstrip at Wake on Sunday, October 15, 1950.[21]

Dwight D. Eisenhower

The election of Dwight D. Eisenhower in 1952 set the stage for a new phase in presidential aviation. During his two terms in office, from 1953 to 1961, the presidential air fleet would continue to expand with new aircraft, including the first jet airliners to be employed by a sitting president.

With the inauguration of Eisenhower came the realization that the *Independence* would have to be retired in favor of a presidential aircraft more attuned to the new administration. Major (later Colonel) William G. Draper, the new presidential pilot, selected a Lockheed Constellation

(C-121A) from the inventory of the 1254th Air Transportation Group stationed at Washington National Airport. Draper had been Eisenhower's pilot in Europe, where he had flown a similar Constellation named the *Columbine*. In the interest of continuity, the new presidential airplane was dubbed the *Columbine II*. The *Columbine II* already had served in an important mission, having flown then President-elect Eisenhower to the Far East in November 1952. Eisenhower had committed himself in the presidential election to seeking a quick end to the Korean War, and his flight in the *Columbine II* shortly thereafter dramatically reinforced his campaign pledge.

The *Columbine II* was a military version of the famed commercial Lockheed airliner model 749, better known as the Lockheed Constellation, or "Connie." It stood apart as

Top: Truman flew on the *Independence* to Wake Island for a meeting with General Douglas MacArthur in October 1950. *Above:* A cartoon shows Truman wearing MacArthur's hat. Drawn by John Churchill, it was published in October 1950, shortly after the Wake Island meeting.

"I settled back and underwent an exhilarating experience—my first jet flight!" Dwight D. Eisenhower

one of the most beautiful commercial airliners of the piston-engine era, a sleek airplane, fast and roomy, the object of considerable affection among air travelers both civilian and military. Ultimately, faster turboprop aircraft and jets replaced the Constellations, but during their heyday they were at the cutting edge of airline service. The speed and range of the Lockheed Constellation stemmed from the fact that the aircraft was fitted with four of the most powerful piston engines in existence, the R-3350 Cyclones.

For service as a presidential airplane, the *Columbine II* was modified in a radical way. A twenty-foot compartment in the waist section was converted into a presidential suite. Two long sofa beds were installed on either side of the

Above: President Eisenhower became a world traveler during his administration, flying on a variety of aircraft, including the first jet transport to be used by a U.S. president.
Opposite: The air force crew for Eisenhower's C-121A Lockheed Constellation, the *Columbine II,* pose next to the presidential plane in November 1953.

stateroom, and a large conference table was placed in the middle of the compartment. At Eisenhower's chair, the designers placed two telephones, one serving as an intercom and the other to be hooked up to a ground link whenever the airplane landed. The private compartment was appointed with a framed picture of columbine blossoms, a small bar, and a cluster of aircraft instruments for the president to monitor during any flight. A galley and lavatory rounded out the design of the interior. The *Columbine II* typically flew with a crew of seven and could carry as many as twenty-four passengers.[22]

In 1954, Eisenhower accepted a new Connie, the *Columbine III,* representing a dramatic upgrade in size, comfort, and technical sophistication. The reasons for the change were many, but the primary factor was the advanced age of the *Columbine II*—it had entered presidential service with more than four thousand hours already recorded on its flight log. The *Columbine III* was an advanced Lockheed design, the "Super Constellation." The VC-121E plane had served briefly as a U.S. Navy aircraft before being transferred to the U.S. Air Force. The new aircraft served for six years before its retirement. The *Columbine III* measured eighteen feet longer than the *Columbine II* and could cruise at a speed of 355 miles per hour.[23]

President Eisenhower became the first chief executive to fly in a jet, traveling to Europe in August 1959 on a trip that included a stop in West Germany for a conference with German chancellor Konrad Adenauer. Eisenhower flew in *Queenie* (VC-137A), a military version of a Boeing 707 jet attached to the 89th Airlift Wing at Andrews. *Queenie* saw only brief service in the presidential fleet, mostly as a backup aircraft. One of its more memorable flights was bringing astronaut John Glenn to Washington in February 1962 after his successful orbiting of Earth.[24]

In his memoirs, Eisenhower observed that his first flight on *Queenie* was a special one in his tenure as president.

"Before departure," he wrote, "I took Mamie aboard to show her the mammoth machine, which was almost completely new to me. Both in size and speed the new airplane completely dwarfed the *Columbine III*, the Super Constellation, that we had considered the last word in luxurious transportation. However, no airplane ever looked attractive to Mamie."[25]

President Eisenhower was an avid air traveler, even if First Lady Mamie Eisenhower never shared his enthusiasm for flight. In fact, he was the first chief executive to have earned his pilot's license while in the military, and he pioneered extensive use of helicopters for shorter jaunts to Andrews Air Force Base for official domestic and foreign flights in his presidential aircraft.

One of the more important historical themes associated

Below: President Eisenhower confers with cabinet members Secretary of the Interior Fred Seaton (*center*) and Secretary of Agriculture Ezra Taft Benson during a flight on the *Columbine III,* January 1957.
Right: First Lady Mamie Eisenhower christens the C-121A *Columbine III* in Washington, D.C., November 1954.

"No airplane ever looked attractive to Mamie." Dwight Eisenhower

President Eisenhower disembarks from one of the first Boeing 707 jets to enter presidential service. The jet transport with the distinctive MATS livery (military air transport service) had flown Eisenhower to Suriname in March 1960.

with the Eisenhower years was the diplomatic initiative to achieve peaceful relations with the Soviet Union. The Eisenhower administration made such diplomacy a high priority. Unfortunately, the ill-fated 1960 summit with Soviet premier Nikita Khrushchev in Paris showcased the tensions of the Cold War. The whole conference was cancelled in the wake of the downing of Francis Gary Powers' U-2 spy plane by the Soviets over their country.

Khrushchev himself had made an extraordinary visit in September 1959 to the United States, landing at Andrews

Air Force Base in a large Tupolev TU-114 airliner. His tour of the United States created a great stir as the irrepressible Soviet leader made the rounds in Washington, D.C., and the hinterlands. During that visit Eisenhower and Khrushchev made a helicopter tour of the capital, but only after the Soviet leader's suspicions were allayed. Unbeknownst to Eisenhower, Khrushchev feared a plot to take him up in a helicopter and throw him to his death.[26] When first offered the helicopter ride, he gave a courteous but firm refusal, stating that he distrusted such machines.

A Crisis Over the North Atlantic
Nikita Khrushchev Encounters a Violent Storm on His Trip to the United States

When Soviet leader Nikita Khrushchev visited the United States in 1959, he chose to fly on one of the Soviet Union's most stunning — and still experimental — airliners, the Tupolev Tu-114. The huge Tu-114 was based on the familiar Cold War symbol of Soviet aviation, the Tu-95 "Bear" bomber, which often patrolled along the North Atlantic to conduct reconnaissance missions on American and British activities at sea.

Soviet planners for the trip — Aeroflot, the KGB, and the Communist Party politburo — expressed great concern because four-fifths of the Moscow-to-Washington journey would be over water. The Soviets rarely took transoceanic flights and therefore lacked training with inflatable rafts, life jackets, and survival techniques at sea. As a precaution, Soviet ships were stationed at two-hundred-mile intervals across the North Atlantic, ready to come to the rescue of the Tu-114 in an emergency. Nervous KGB agents even built a mock-up of the fuselage and tested it in a large swimming pool in Moscow.

Despite all the anxiety in Soviet officialdom, the flight to America went well, setting the stage for Khrushchev to make a whirlwind tour of the United States. Only on the Tu-114's return flight, while entering the North Atlantic on the homeward leg near Greenland, did trouble arise in the form of a violent and prolonged storm. Leonid Kerber, a crew member, tells in his memoir of "tongues of blue flame streaming along the windshield. It was as if the propeller spinners and tips of the blades were on fire, and the trains of fire flowed off them into space."[27] The pointers on the magnetic and radio compasses moved erratically. Worst of

Above: Soviet leader Nikita Khrushchev (*second from right*) arrives at Idlewild (today JFK) International Airport in New York for his historic visit to the United States in 1959.
Left: Khrushchev flew to the United States on an impressive Tupolev Tu-114 airliner with its four powerful turboprop engines.

all, radio communication with Moscow was lost.

While Khrushchev slept quietly, the Tu-114 flew through the sudden magnetic storm, a phenomenon often called "St. Elmo's fire." Kerber and crew made the decision not to wake the Soviet leader. But they did fear that Moscow might interpret his radio silence as evidence of a catastrophe or some act of treachery by the United States. The episode passed without news coverage, but nevertheless represented an anxious moment in the history of the Cold War.

The Tupolev Tu-114 impressed Americans with its huge size and range. The Tu-114 design was a civilian adaptation of the Tu-95 Bear bomber, which, at the time, made routine aerial reconnaissance flights in the North Atlantic.

"Whether you like it or not

АЭРОФ Л

"...history is on our side. We will bury you." **Nikita Khrushchev**

Close Calls on Air Force One

Rare Moments in Presidential Air Travel When Things Go Wrong

Air Force One enjoys a well-deserved reputation for safety. Over the decades, presidential air travel has been animated by the highest standards of aircraft maintenance and crew training. Glistening presidential planes, embodying the latest in technology, have operated globally with an exemplary record for flight safety. American presidents have routinely flown hundreds of thousands of miles without technical mishaps. But there have been a few anxious moments.

While en route from the 1943 Tehran conference, flying on a U.S. Army Air Force C-54 transport, Franklin Roosevelt faced potential disaster on a landing approach to Malta. The presidential plane's flaps, the extensions of the wing that serve as a brake, did not release and fall into position. This meant a high-speed landing for the plane, with a runway crater or tire failure inviting disaster. When told of the problem, Roosevelt merely tightened his seat belts and watched the unfolding landing from his window seat, displaying considerable serenity in the face of the emergency. Hitting the runway at 150 miles an hour, a touchdown speed well above normal, the cockpit crew still managed to maneuver the plane to a safe stop. Without fanfare, FDR quietly disembarked from his plane to complete his scheduled itinerary.[28]

In February 1945, Roosevelt traveled by air to the Yalta conference in the Crimea. On board the *Sacred Cow*, with Major Henry T. Myers as pilot in command, the president encountered an unforeseen crisis. Once in Soviet air space, Major Myers spotted a Russian plane in the direct flight path of the *Sacred Cow*. An escort of P-51 fighters hovered nearby, offering protection for the presiden-

President Dwight Eisenhower's Boeing 707 at Suriname in South America after an unscheduled stop prompted by engine failure. This particular jet, one of three in a VIP pool, was known by its call sign SAM 970 or its informal name *Queenie.*

tial plane. When the escort leader saw the approaching Russian plane, he perceived it as a threat and ordered an attack. Myers quickly countermanded the order, keenly aware that a dogfight would not be an optimal way to herald the arrival of Roosevelt for the Yalta conference. In the face of the danger, Myers promptly dove one thousand feet to ensure that the *Sacred Cow* was not on the same flight path as the Soviet plane. The pilot of the Soviet aircraft did not alter his heading or altitude, suggesting that he was unaware of the challenge he had posed to the presidential plane.[29]

Fifteen years later, Dwight Eisenhower experienced a flight emergency on SAM 970, the Boeing

707 jet used occasionally by the White House for extended travel. Eisenhower made a high-profile trip to Latin America in early 1960, a diplomatic gesture to restate America's goodwill policy at a time when Fidel Castro's revolutionary regime in Cuba was openly challenging American interests. On March 2, while above the Amazon jungle on a flight path from Montevideo to Puerto Rico, one of the four engines on the president's plane broke down. Major William G. Draper, Eisenhower's pilot, responded by putting SAM 970 on a landing path to nearby Paramaribo, Suriname, on the northern coast of South America, where Eisenhower and his party were then transferred to another plane for the return flight to Washington, D.C.[30]

The history of Air Force One has been punctuated by occasional mishaps, but none has led to catastrophe, a remarkable record in more than six decades of presidential flying.

"But while riding with him from the airport that morning," Eisenhower recorded in his memoirs, "I deliberately expressed my regret that he could not join me on this kind of sightseeing, for I had found them convenient and always interesting. 'Oh,' he replied, 'if you are to be in the same helicopter, of course, I will go!'"[31]

Khrushchev has left us some fleeting images of presidential travel in the Eisenhower years. In his memoir, *Khrushchev Remembers,* he described how at the Geneva summit of 1955 the American presidential aircraft outclassed the Soviet planes. "Unfortunately, our own delegation," Khrushchev observed, "found itself at a disadvantage from the very moment we arrived at the Geneva airport. The leaders of the other three delegations arrived in four-engine planes, and we arrived in a modest two-engine Ilyushin IL-14. Their planes were more impressive than ours, and the comparison was somewhat embarrassing."[32] Thus, when Khrushchev visited the United States in 1959 he came in an impressive chariot of his own, the Tupolev TU-114, a symbol of Soviet triumphs in the design of large airliners.

One of the most bizarre episodes of the Cold War related to Eisenhower's proposed trip to the Soviet Union in May 1960. The plan called for the installation of cameras on the presidential plane, to be activated manually over Soviet territory. The elegant plan never came to fruition because of the collapse of the Paris summit that same month, in the wake of the U-2 incident. Eisenhower was to fly to Moscow following the summit. The clandestine scheme was never disclosed to him. The hidden cameras were to be activated in the cockpit, with the on-off switch cleverly concealed in the ordinary instrumentation and controls. The elaborate effort to conceal the camera controls was necessary because the Soviets required one of their own representatives in the cockpit on the approach to Moscow.[33]

Nikita Khrushchev boards an American military helicopter for an aerial tour of Washington, D.C., with President Eisenhower in July 1959.

The mid-century administrations of Franklin Roosevelt, Harry Truman, and Dwight Eisenhower signaled the arrival of the Air Age at the White House. Each of these presidents made full and efficient use of the airplane as a mode of travel. With each passing decade, of course, the airplane became more and more central to the operation of the American presidency — a reality that became clear to all during the 1960s.

Chapter Three The Jet Age
John F. Kennedy and Lyndon B. Johnson

THE TURBULENT DECADE of the 1960s marked a new phase in presidential air travel. The acquisition of a jet transport for the exclusive use of the chief executive represented a new level of modernity in flight operations for the White House. The call sign "Air Force One" acquired widespread use, entering the popular lexicon as an enduring symbol of the American presidency.

The election of John F. Kennedy in 1960 set the stage for the modernization of White House flight operations. On October 10, 1962, the 1254th Air Transport Wing (forerunner of the 89th Airlift Wing) took possession of a special-order Boeing 707-353B airliner. This was the first jet specifically designated for presidential use. The new plane carried the designation VC-137C (Special Air Mission, or SAM 26000) and joined a pool of other VIP aircraft set aside for the transport of high-ranking government officials, cabinet officers, and congressmen on official business. Eventually SAM 26000 became synonymous in the popular mind with Air Force One, although the designator "Air Force One" could and did apply to any air force plane carrying the president of the United States.

President Kennedy flew on SAM 26000 for only one

Opposite: President Kennedy and First Lady Jackie Kennedy disembark from Air Force One at Love Field, Dallas, Texas, on November 22, 1963. *Above:* Upon arrival at Love Field, the Kennedys greeted a crowd of enthusiastic supporters. The first lady is shown with the president, holding a bouquet of flowers.

year, often making use of other aircraft assigned to the presidential wing at Andrews Air Force Base. Before 1962, Kennedy used one of the three executive jet transports that had entered the inventory during the Eisenhower administration. These modified Boeing 707-153s, designated by the air force as VC-137A, were purchased from Boeing in 1959. Unlike SAM 26000, these three jets were not designated presidential planes.

Kennedy also made extensive use of an Air Force C-118A Liftmaster, a modified DC-6A piston-powered airliner, which remained in presidential service until 1967. Similar to Harry Truman's *Independence,* the C-118A offered Kennedy a private compartment for his family, plus an office with desk and swivel chair and seating for advisers. Often this was the aircraft of choice to carry the president to his home in Hyannis Port, Massachusetts.

With the advent of SAM 26000, however, First Lady Jacqueline Kennedy, with the enthusiastic collaboration of her husband, decided to give presidential travel a stylish new look, enlisting the famed industrial designer Raymond Loewy to create a new livery for the presidential aircraft. Loewy made extensive use of blue, white, and silver to

Right: First Lady Jacqueline Kennedy greets a well-wisher shortly after disembarking from Air Force One. Two hours later, on this tragic day, President Kennedy would be assassinated in Dealey Plaza in downtown Dallas. *Opposite:* Those who came to Love Field on November 22, 1963, were corralled behind a fence, as seen here. Air Force One provides a backdrop as the president and first lady shake hands with their supporters in the crowd.

transform the exterior of SAM 26000, creating its trademark Air Force One paint scheme. A veteran designer, Loewy had fashioned the sleek lines of the Studebaker Avanti sports car, several streamlined engines of the Pennsylvania Railroad, and a host of designs for well-known corporate clients such as Coca-Cola, Ritz Crackers, and Lucky Strike cigarettes.

The stunning new Air Force One fit well into the youthful imagery associated with the Kennedy administration, offering a stylish winged expression of Camelot. Indelible images of President Kennedy and the airplane persist in our collective historical memory: Air Force One served as a backdrop for the president and first lady as they greeted well-wishers at Dallas's Love Field on the morning of November 22, 1963, and later that same day became an

improvised hearse that brought the body of the slain president home to Washington. Arguably no aircraft has ever been etched so powerfully on the national consciousness.

SAM 26000 began its thirty-five-year service career two days after its arrival at Andrews, when it was flown to Libya to bring the country's crown prince to the United States for a state visit. A month later, on November 12, President Kennedy made his first flight on the airplane, a short trip to New York to attend the funeral of former first lady Eleanor Roosevelt. The new presidential airplane established a benchmark in May 1963 while flying an American delegation from Washington to Moscow, a flight that set a new nonstop speed record. Kennedy made dramatic use of SAM 26000 in June 1963, flying to Berlin to make his famous "Ich Bin Ein Berliner" speech at the height of the Cold War.

For the thousand days of his administration, President Kennedy faced formidable challenges in the sphere of international affairs. In his 1961 inaugural address, Kennedy stated, "Let every nation know, whether it wishes us well or ill, that we shall pay any price, bear any burden, meet any hardship, support any friend, oppose any foe, in order to assure the survival and the success of liberty."[1]

Kennedy experienced the compelling need to engage the Soviet Union and its client states on several fronts, a policy that set the stage for direct confrontations with Soviet leader Nikita Khrushchev over the status of West Berlin in 1961 and the placement of Soviet nuclear-tipped missiles in Cuba in 1962. The latter conflict represented a major triumph for the youthful president, but the Cuban Missile Crisis nonetheless had taken a reluctant world to the brink of nuclear war. No less important for the future, Kennedy also set the stage for American involvement in the Vietnam War by sending thousands of military advisers to assist the South Vietnamese Army in its struggle against communist guerrillas.

"It's magnificent! I'll take it." John F. Kennedy

The First Lady and the Industrial Designer

Raymond Loewy Gives Air Force One a Stylish New Look

President John F. Kennedy twice met with the famed industrial designer Raymond Loewy in 1962. The encounter of an American president with one of the most innovative designers of the twentieth century led to an important collaboration, one that would ultimately transform the appearance of Air Force One.

Loewy came to the White House after convincing a Kennedy aide that the existing paint scheme for the presidential plane was ugly in the extreme: at the time, few would have contested Loewy's assertion that the plane's telltale military look (adorned with dabs of high-visibility orange paint) was not the ideal image for the American presidency. First Lady Jacqueline Kennedy, a person keenly interested in questions of design, endorsed the Loewy critique. She then became a strong advocate for the adoption of a stylish new livery for Air Force One.[2]

Loewy possessed impressive credentials as a designer and was a man of considerable influence. Born in France, Loewy had moved to the United States in 1922. His quick rise in the design world was remarkable, from poverty to ownership of the largest design firm in New York by the end of the 1940s. By the time of his meetings with Kennedy, Loewy's portfolio included memorable design work on streamlined trains and their interiors, Lucky Strike cigarettes, Coca-Cola dispensers, Hallicrafter radios, stylish clothing, refrigerators, and Studebaker cars. Later in life, Loewy described his work in industrial design as a "simple exercise — a little logic, a little taste, and the will to cooperate."[3]

When Loewy met with President Kennedy in

Industrial designer Raymond Loewy appeared on the cover of the October 31, 1949, issue of *Time* magazine. Loewy's international fame prompted the Kennedys to invite him to design a new paint scheme for Air Force One.

May 1962 he spent an interlude on the floor of the Oval Office, working with colored paper and crayons, to sketch out for the president his ideas for a new paint scheme for Air Force One.[4] The designer enjoyed the confidence and high expectations of the Kennedy White House.

Prior to Loewy's work, Kennedy himself had made certain interim steps to alter the appearance of presidential planes, ordering the removal of distinct military lettering such as "U.S. Air Force" or "MATS" (Military Air Transport Service) in favor the simple designation "United States of America." For Kennedy, the shift to nonmilitary nomencla-

ture suggested the national character of presidential planes.

Loewy's design reflected Kennedy's preference for the use of blue. The designer's proposed livery for Air Force One was elegant, fully utilizing the hues of blue, white, and silver. The plane was emblazoned with the presidential seal and the words "United States of America" on the side of the fuselage. This striking design on SAM 26000 became the familiar image of the flying White House. The Loewy design, in turn, cast a long shadow — all subsequent Air Force One planes bear this distinctive paint scheme, including the current 747s in presidential service.

The impact of the new livery was immediate and powerful for all who saw Air Force One. *Time* magazine reporter Hugh Sidey accompanied the Kennedys on one of their high-profile trips to France. Sidey and the press contingent arrived ahead of the president and were afforded a chance to see the landing of Air Force One in its new colors. As the presidential plane taxied across the rain-soaked tarmac at Paris, all were impressed with its new look, for Sidey a testament to the sense of style and spectacle that the president and his first lady had brought to the White House. With the sunlight breaking through the clouds and glistening on the plane, Sidey reported that Air Force One served as a stunning backdrop for the presidential visit. Such a feat, in his view, reflected the influence of Jacqueline Kennedy, who had hired Raymond Loewy.[5]

Later in life, Loewy accepted the commission to work on the design of a memorial postage stamp in honor of the slain president, the designer's collaborator on the paint scheme for Air Force One.

Above: Raymond Loewy ponders a model with his design for a new Air Force One paint scheme.

Left: The contrast of the old and new can be seen in these photos of a Boeing 707, first with the air force transport markings in orange and silver and second with the inspired Loewy design that endures to this day.

JFK's Ailments
The Hidden Health Crisis of Camelot

President John F. Kennedy was to his contemporaries the embodiment of youthful activism. Though he was known to have a bad back, most Americans assumed Kennedy was in good health. This image of vitality persisted during Kennedy's tenure as president and beyond. Recently, however, historian Robert Dallek and physician Jeffrey A. Kelman gained exclusive access to the late president's medical records; their assessment of Kennedy's health in the last eight years of his life tells another story.

The medical records reveal a president in chronic pain, beleaguered by many ailments and dependent on a variety of medications, including painkillers, anti-anxiety drugs, stimulants, antibiotics, sleeping pills, and a battery of medications to combat colitis, urinary track infections, and adrenal insufficiency. Kennedy labored under the effects of Addison's disease, a life-threatening deficiency of the adrenal function. In addition, the pain in his back muscles was sometimes severe enough to require injections.

Few photos have survived to challenge the enduring image of Kennedy in robust health. However, an image captured in 1961, showing Kennedy being hoisted in a steel cage to the entrance of Air Force One, hinted at the concealed health problems. At the time, few realized that this extraordinary technique for entering the presidential plane reflected a world leader coping with severe illness.[6]

According to those who worked around the president and to historian Dallek, Kennedy's health problems never seemed to have compromised his ability to function as chief executive.

President John Kennedy is lifted by crane for his entrance into Air Force One at Andrews Air Force Base, a measure taken to make boarding the presidential plane easier for the chronically ill president.

First with President Eisenhower and then with his successor, Kennedy, national security had dictated that a modern president make optimal use of jet technology for conferences and state visits on a global scale. Air Force One thus became an essential arm of presidential leadership.

A Fateful Day in Dallas

When not engaged by international crises, Kennedy sought to employ his beautiful Air Force One for domestic purposes, which set the stage for a five-city tour of Texas in the fall of 1963. For the crew of Air Force One, there was no inkling that this journey to the American Southwest would place their elegant jet transport at the epicenter of a national tragedy.

One primary motive for the trip to Texas was the desire by the White House staff to strengthen Kennedy's political base in the home state of his vice president, Lyndon B. Johnson. Both men realized that Texas, with its twenty-five electoral votes, would be a key player in the coming 1964 election. By late September, presidential adviser Kenneth O'Donnell had finalized the itinerary for the Texas trip with the U.S. Secret Service: President Kennedy would visit five Texas cities between November 21 and 23, ending with a night's rest at LBJ's Texas ranch before returning to Washington. Before the journey ended, Kennedy would have an opportunity to speak to tens of thousands of Texans. A motorcade through downtown Dallas at midday on Friday, November 22, was designed to be a culminating moment for the political trip.

The fast-paced itinerary called for Air Force One to bring President Kennedy and First Lady Jacqueline Kennedy to Dallas's Love Field at 11:35 A.M. After a short interlude to shake hands with onlookers at the edge of the tarmac, Kennedy and his party would leave promptly for downtown Dallas. The departure time for the motorcade was 11:45 A.M., with an anticipated 12:30 P.M. arrival at

the Trade Mart for a luncheon sponsored by the Dallas Citizens Council. The Secret Service planned to return the presidential party to Love Field by no later than 2:30 P.M. Five minutes later, as projected in the precise schedule, Air Force One would take off for the final leg of the journey, a short flight to Austin. Two other planes were part of the official party: Vice President Johnson and his wife, Lady Bird Johnson, flew on Air Force Two with Texas governor John Connelly and other local dignitaries; a third plane transported the press corps covering the event.

The Kennedy motorcade made its way through downtown Dallas in a deliberate way, moving down Houston Street with cheering crowds hugging the curbs on both sides of the thoroughfare, and then turning at a sharp 120-degree angle onto Elm Street. The president was seated in an open Lincoln presidential limousine. On this Friday afternoon with a glaring sun above, the plastic canopy for the limousine had been removed to allow the Dallas citizenry to see the president. The red brick Texas School Book Depository, situated above a grassy knoll on Dealey

Below: President Kennedy in his limousine in Dealey Plaza, Dallas, Texas, just moments before he was shot. In the car with the president are First Lady Jacqueline Kennedy and Governor and Mrs. John Connelly of Texas.

Moments after President Kennedy was mortally wounded, Secret Service agent Clinton Hill leaps into the presidential limousine as it speeds toward Parkland Hospital.

"Suddenly, there was an explosive noise — distinct, sharp, resounding." Rufus Youngblood, Secret Service

Plaza, towered over Elm Street on the right side. Seated to the left of the president in the rear seat was Jacqueline Kennedy, dressed in a pink two-piece wool suit; a bouquet of roses rested between them. Governor Connelly and his wife, Nellie, were seated in the jump seats immediately in front of the president and the first lady.

With the Trade Mart just minutes away, there was a sudden clap of gunfire, followed by two more shots. Rufus Youngblood, a Secret Service agent accompanying Vice President Johnson, remembered vividly the scene in Dealey Plaza: "Suddenly, there was an explosive noise — distinct, sharp, resounding. Nothing that could be mistaken for the incessant popping and backfiring of the motorcycles, but in the instant I heard it I could not be certain if it had been a firecracker, bullet, bomb, or some other explosive. I looked around quickly and saw nothing to indicate its source."[7]

From behind the presidential motorcade, at a distance of eighty-eight yards, Lee Harvey Oswald had fired three shots from the sixth floor of the Book Depository. The first shot missed the motorcade. Oswald's second shot hit Kennedy in the back, exited from his throat, and then passed through Connelly's back and chest, striking the governor's wrist. The third shot, after the lapse of a mere five seconds, struck the president on the right side of his head. Kennedy had been killed instantly, but emergency room doctors at nearby Parkland Hospital tried vainly to revive him. The president was declared dead at 1 P.M. Dallas time.

The assassin, Lee Harvey Oswald, would be apprehended later in the afternoon. At the time, however, the Secret Service had no knowledge of Oswald's role or, for that matter, any firm grasp of what had transpired in Dealey Plaza. Logical fears of a widespread conspiracy cast a shadow over every move they made. Protection for the new president, Lyndon Johnson, now became paramount.

Vice President Lyndon B. Johnson leaves Parkland Hospital in the immediate aftermath of the Kennedy assassination on November 22, 1963. Johnson rushed to Love Field, where, on Air Force One, he was sworn in as president of the United States.

No less a concern was the compelling need to provide security for Mrs. Kennedy, still at the hospital and determined not to leave Dallas without the body of her deceased husband.

In this context of mounting confusion and uncertainty, Air Force One moved to center stage as an extension of the White House, offering a logical place of refuge, a secure communications link to the outside world, and a quick means to escape Dallas for the more familiar environs of Washington. There was some discussion of moving the plane to Carswell Air Force base in nearby Fort Worth, on the assumption that a military facility would offer greater security, but this option was eventually rejected in favor of keeping Air Force One at Love Field with added security. During the uncertain hours after the assassination, the Secret Service used the presidential plane as a pivot for their hurried and improvised plans to gain some mastery over the unfolding events of the day.[8]

Colonel James Swindal, the pilot of Air Force One, had not left the airplane during the motorcade into Dallas. Since the presidential party was to return to Love Field in a short span of time, he attended to preparations for the next leg of the Texas trip. While monitoring the radio traffic among the Secret Service agents on the motorcade, at around 12:30 P.M. Swindal heard the crackle of loud voices and shouts, followed by silence, the telltale signs of a crisis. After a long interlude, there was a telephone call to Swindal from Brigadier General Godfrey McHugh, President Kennedy's air force aide, who was at Parkland Hospital. General McHugh ordered him to refuel Air Force One immediately, cancel the old flight plan to Austin, and file a new plan for a direct return to Washington.[9]

As the Secret Service attempted to gain control over the crisis, Merriman Smith of United Press International, who had been in the Kennedy motorcade, promptly dictated the

Air Force One (SAM 26000) returns to Washington, D.C., on November 22, 1963, in this cutaway sketch from the February 21, 1967, issue of *Look* magazine. Note the casket of the slain president at the tail of the airplane.

first bulletin to the outside world over the press car's radio telephone: "Three shots were fired at President Kennedy's motorcade in downtown Dallas." This chilling news flash swept across the nation and alerted the outside world to the assassination.

On board Air Force One, crowded around a television in the president's cabin, Colonel Swindal and the crew heard the news that Kennedy had been shot. Television offered other Americans as well a steady stream of news from Dallas on that Friday afternoon, stunning the country.

Lyndon Johnson, initially trapped in the chaotic environs of Parkland Hospital, accepted the urgent recommendation of the Secret Service that he return to the safety of Air Force One. Secret Service agent Youngblood, who had thrown Johnson to the floor of his limousine when the initial volley of shots broke out, called Air Force One on his walkie-talkie radio, alerting the crew that they were on their way.

The specter of a conspiracy dominated the thoughts of Youngblood and the rest of the Secret Service contingent as they sped through the streets of Dallas toward Love Field. Riding in the car with LBJ, Youngblood was greatly relieved as his car swerved onto the tarmac at the airport: "Suddenly there before us was one of the most welcome sights I have ever seen — the big, gleaming blue and white jet, with UNITED STATES OF AMERICA painted along the fuselage above the long row of windows and the number 26000 gracing the tail rudder."[10]

Writing years later, President Johnson told of the hurried passage to Love Field to board Air Force One: "Secret Service men rushed through the interior ahead of us, pulling down the shades and closing both doors behind us. . . . I realized that the staff of the Secret Service had been right in insisting that I go to Air Force One immediately. That plane is the closest thing to a traveling White House that man can devise. It affords the personnel, the security, and the communications equipment a President must have to do his job."[11]

In preparation for the hurried departure of Air Force One, Swindal had ordered the ground air conditioner disconnected. When Johnson arrived at 1:33 P.M., the plane was already heating up under the rays of the afternoon Texas sun. Now functioning as president, Johnson began to assert his control over the situation, ordering that President Kennedy's private cabin at the rear of the plane be reserved for Mrs. Kennedy, who would soon join him aboard the presidential airplane at Love Field. Later, Johnson spoke of that altered reality when for the first time he greeted the assembled staff on Air Force One: "It was at that moment that I realized nothing would ever be the same again. A wall — high, forbidding, historic — separated us now, a wall that derived from the Office of the Presidency of the United States." Henceforth all the Kennedy and Johnson staffers were to address him as "Mr. President."[12]

"Nothing would ever be the same again. A wall separated us now.

derived from the **Office of the Presidency of the United States."**
Lyndon B. Johnson

"The greatest leader of our time has been struck down by the foulest deed of our time." Lyndon B. Johnson

White House reporter Merriman Smith heard the formal announcement of Kennedy's death in a conference room at Parkland Hospital. Before Smith had ample time to confront his own emotions or relay the announcement to the outside world, he found himself on another mission: White House staffers summoned him to Air Force One for the flight back to Washington. Smith, as it turned out, was one of two reporters selected to make up the press pool for this historic trip home. Escorted by the Secret Service on a fast drive to Love Field, he arrived at the airport in time to witness the swearing in of Lyndon Johnson as President of United States.

"Aboard Air Force One," Smith remembered, "all the shades of the larger main cabin had been drawn and the interior was hot and dimly lighted." Ushered into the cabin, the reporter found himself wedged just inside the door, one of twenty-seven people crowded into the small space. Johnson and his wife, Lady Bird, stood in the center. Next to Johnson was U.S. District Judge Sarah T. Hughes, who had been hurriedly brought to the plane for the swearing-in ceremony.[13]

The assembled group included Kennedy and Johnson staff members, congressmen, members of the aircraft crew, and Secret Service agents. They waited patiently in the oppressive heat for the appearance of Jacqueline Kennedy, who had boarded Air Force One just moments before. All eyes turned to the first lady as she entered the cabin. "She appeared alone," Smith observed, "dressed in the same pink wool suit she had worn in the morning when she appeared so happy shaking hands with airport crowds at the side of her husband. She was white faced but dry-eyed. Friendly hands stretched toward her as she stumbled slightly. Johnson took both of her hands in his and motioned her to his left side. Lady Bird stood on his right, a fixed half smile showing the tension."[14]

The two-minute swearing-in ceremony signaled the formal transfer of power. The new president turned to kiss his wife, and then hugged Jacqueline Kennedy and kissed her on the cheek. After some awkward expressions of best wishes, the president ordered, "Now, let's get airborne."

The newly sworn-in president could not have flown out of Dallas without Mrs. Kennedy on board. There was no question of leaving her in Dallas with the body of her slain husband: they were to return to Washington on Air Force One. However, few on board the plane at that moment realized the difficulties the Secret Service had faced in delivering the first lady to Love Field with the body of the deceased president.

While at Parkland Hospital, Kennedy advisers, backed up by the Secret Service contingent that had arrived in the wake of the assassination, faced a challenge from Dr. Earl Rose, the Dallas County Medical Examiner. Rose argued that because the Kennedy death had been a homicide, the body could not be removed pending an autopsy. He rejected the repeated overtures from agitated Secret Service agents, O'Donnell, and the other Kennedy staffers gathered at Parkland. Mrs. Kennedy was anxious to leave for Love Field, and she lingered impatiently in an adjoining hospital room as the furor unfolded.

Despite repeated appeals, Dr. Rose remained unyielding; he even rejected the desperate ploy of O'Donnell and company to accompany the casket to Washington on Air Force One. Finally, O'Donnell announced, "We're leaving," and ordered that the casket be wheeled out to the awaiting ambulance. With Mrs. Kennedy, the group boldly dashed out and sped off to Love Field.[15]

The Air Force One crew had worked swiftly to prepare the aircraft for the reception of the casket. The idea of placing the corpse of the slain president in the hold of the aircraft was rejected out of hand. The only alternative was to place it in the rear passenger compartment, which required some instant hands-on redesign of the relatively small space. A partition was removed, along with four seats, to allow the casket easy entry and placement. It took no small amount of energy to move the nine-hundred-pound bronze casket up the narrow ramp into the compartment, where it rested across from the galley. It would be here that Mrs. Kennedy chose to seat herself, surrounded by a host of her husband's former staff, for the long flight home.

By the time Air Force One departed, news of the Kennedy assassination had spread widely, even to the most remote parts of the country. Presidential historian and reporter Theodore White aptly described news reports of the event as "a clap of alarm as sharp and startling as the memory of Pearl Harbor," as radio, television, and word of mouth quickly reported the inexplicable fate of an American president in Dallas. He observed, "Television switchboards clotted within hours. Some parents tugged little children directly to church; others lowered the flag over their green lawns of suburbia. Taxi drivers caught by red lights in city traffic passed the latest bulletin from one to another. In New York a young woman was driving up Manhattan's East River Drive when her car radio reported that the President had been shot; when she reached the toll gate of the Triborough Bridge, a detail of guards had just left their stations and were lowering the flag to half-staff. . . . One student hit a tree with his fist; another lay on his stomach — he was crying. Uncontrollably, across the country, men sobbed in the streets of cities and did not have to explain why."[16]

Against this backdrop, Colonel Swindal lifted Air Force One off the runway at Love Field for the flight to Washington. News accounts alerted the nation to the flight and the anticipated landing of the presidential plane at Andrews Air Force Base in the early evening. The plane was cleared for a cruising altitude of 29,000 feet, but Swindal decided to climb another 12,000 feet before leveling off

and establishing a cruising speed of 625 miles per hour. Air Force One was favored with a strong tailwind for its melancholy aerial trek home. Along with his co-pilot, Lieutenant Colonel Lewis Hanson, and the crew, Colonel Swindal felt a strong sense of urgency to get to Washington as soon as possible. The attention of the nation now focused intently on one airplane on its long flight homeward.

White captured the scene on the ground in the nation's capital as Air Force One sped home: "Through the gathering dusk of a moist and balmy Washington evening — the sky broken, the gray cloud bars washed pink by the setting sun — the black government limousines, the private cars, the taxis, raced to Andrews Air Force Base."[17] Small clusters of people gathered along the anticipated route of the ambulance bearing the president's body, from Andrews Air Force Base in the Maryland suburbs to the District of Columbia.

Air Force One finally landed at 6:05 P.M., completing

Upon hearing the news of the assassination of President Kennedy, an unidentified woman expresses her grief on a street in Washington, D.C.

"I will do my best. That is all that I can do. I ask for your help — and God's." Lyndon B. Johnson

a flight of two hours and eighteen minutes from Dallas. Scores of news reporters and hundreds of VIPs greeted the plane as it taxied to a stop in the reception area. Attorney General Robert Kennedy, the brother of the slain president, boarded the plane to be with Jacqueline Kennedy for the arrival ceremonies. Under glare of lights, television cameras conveyed to a stunned nation the dramatic moment when the bronze casket was transferred to a gray U.S. Navy ambulance. Mrs. Kennedy and her brother-in-law, joined by a small contingent of personal aides and Secret Service agents, climbed into the ambulance. With its red dome light flashing, the ambulance, escorted by four black limousines, drove off into the evening darkness for Bethesda Naval Hospital. Later, an autopsy would be performed at this renowned medical facility, a crucial step in the long process of investigating the assassination in Dallas.

In the shadow of Air Force One, President Lyndon Johnson walked to a cluster of floodlit microphones and told the nation: "I will do my best. That is all that I can do. I ask your help — and God's."

Lyndon B. Johnson

The martyrdom of John Kennedy had bequeathed to the new president a powerful mandate, which provided extraordinary leverage in domestic affairs. Already known for his legislative skills as the former Senate majority leader, Lyndon Johnson pushed through Congress the landmark Civil Rights Act of 1964, which he argued was a fitting memorial to the fallen president. That same year, he won election in his own right in a landslide victory over Republican candidate Barry Goldwater.

In foreign affairs, President Johnson was pro-active and not given to any hesitancy in the face of the communist expansion is Southeast Asia. He quickly increased America's military involvement in the Vietnam War in a fateful

Opposite: **Now sworn in as president, Lyndon B. Johnson addresses the nation at Andrews Air Force Base on the evening of November 22, 1963, making a brief statement to the press and the public.**
Below: **President Johnson confers with Congressman Rodney Love on a flight to the Midwest in September 1966.**

way during the first six months of 1965, steadily accelerating American force to help defend the Republic of South Vietnam against guerrilla insurgents sponsored and led by Ho Chi Minh, the leader of communist North Vietnam. By the end of his tenure in office, Johnson had committed more than 500,000 American troops to the war effort.

The war proved to be a prolonged and bloody affair, in which American conventional arms — and even significant victories on the ground — failed to bring about a favorable military solution. In the face of this stalemate, opposition at home mounted dramatically, forcing Johnson to abandon his plans to seek reelection in 1968. On March 31 of that year, the president stunned the nation when he announced in a television address: "I shall not seek, and I will not accept, the nomination of my party for another term as your president." Thus, Lyndon Johnson himself became a casualty of the Vietnam War, a conflict that would continue for another five years.

During his years in office President Johnson made extensive use of Air Force One, for travels to Vietnam and other countries. And on one remarkable occasion he made an around-the-world journey, seemingly more on impulse than purposes of state. Often he called SAM 26000 "my own little plane," and he was adept at offering rides on the fabled airplane to impress or reward people, an unparalleled perk in the political currency of his time. In addition to Air Force One, LBJ flew in a Convair VC-131H Samaritan, a twin-engine turboprop with a silver and white livery, for shorter trips out of Washington or to visit his ranch in Texas. At Bergstrom Air Force Base in Austin, President and Lady Bird Johnson also made use of a small Air Force Beech VC-6A twin-engine aircraft for shuttle flights from the air base to the Johnson ranch.

Significant alterations to SAM 26000 took place during the Johnson years to reflect the personality and ego of the new chief executive. LBJ ordered additional seats to be installed and had certain rows of seats reconfigured to face the rear of the airplane so that eyes focused backward

Above, left: Lyndon Johnson relaxes with staff and guests on an Air Force One flight in November 1966. The clear partition behind LBJ allowed him to see down the length of the plane.
Right: President Johnson, at the apogee of his power and influence, is joined for a flight on Air Force One by a group of congressmen. Johnson sits in his special seat.
Opposite: Another interior view of Air Force One during the Johnson years, showing the president meeting with a delegation from New York on a flight in March 1966.

toward the president's cabin. He also removed the cherry wood partitions separating the passengers from the stateroom and replaced them with clear plastic ones. All these modifications accented the centrality of Johnson on any flight and, at the same time, allowed the president to observe closely his flying entourage.[18]

One key structural change on Air Force One was the installation of what the Secret Service called the "throne" (dubbed by the press corps the "king's chair"). A spacious leather chair with a high back, it was positioned behind a half-crescent table. Facing his advisers, seated on the opposite side of the table, the president had the option of lowering or raising the table by means of a switch. By virtue of positioning the table, he could assume a towering and intimidating presence over his advisers and guests seated around the "throne." Johnson used this area for frequent conferences, often over lunch, where he could — and usually did — dominate any conversation on the presidential plane. The chief executive often occupied the observer's seat in the cockpit, which afforded

On a trip to Australia, President Johnson speaks to Australian prime minister Harold Holt (*far right*) in October 1966. Lady Bird Johnson is seated third from the left.

"The magic carpet has a way of intoxicating presidents, imparting a sense of power every bit as real as the jet engines outside the cabin windows." Ralph Albertazzie, presidential pilot

him a chance to talk to the pilot and crew while in flight.

In their book *The Flying White House,* reporter Jerald terHorst and presidential pilot Ralph Albertazzie articulated arguably the best summation of what they called Johnson's "all-embracing" style: "The magic carpet has a way of intoxicating presidents, imparting a sense of power every bit as real as the jet engines outside the cabin windows. One moment he could be earthy, profane, selfish, devious, or rude, and then polite, considerate, affectionate, and downright charming. Whatever his mood, it was usually excessive."[19]

President Johnson twice used Air Force One, in 1966 and 1967, to visit American troops in Vietnam. His journeys to the war zone took place against a backdrop of the growing anti-war movement at home. But for Johnson, the treks to Vietnam offered a chance to reaffirm the legitimacy of the war and to boost the morale of the American military. Visiting the huge military base at Cam Ranh Bay on his 1966 tour, Johnson reviewed the troops, talked to many servicemen, and signed countless autographs. Other diplomatic stops on his seventeen-day Asian tour on SAM 26000 included the Philippines, Thailand, Malaysia, and South Korea.

In his memoir, Johnson wrote that he found the trip to be exhausting physically and emotionally, but asserted that the flight on SAM 26000 to the war zone had allowed him a chance to see one major military base up close. "I wanted to visit our fighting men," he wrote. "I wanted to tell them how their president and most of their countrymen felt about what they were doing. I have never been more moved by any group I have talked to, never in my life."[20] However, LBJ's dramatic foray into the war zone had little, if any, impact on the course of the war. Moreover, the trip failed to reverse the steady decline in public support of the war and confidence in President Johnson's leadership.

The following year, Johnson made one of the most bizarre presidential trips in history when he impulsively went aloft on a largely unplanned around-the-world aerial odyssey. The trip — seemingly for no legitimate political purpose — became a source of bitter complaint among the press corps who found themselves caught up in the vortex of the president's wanderlust. Arguably, at no time in the history of the Johnson presidency would the press corps be so at odds with the chief executive or more critical of his apparent megalomania.

Boarding Air Force One on December 19, 1967,

Below, left: On a world tour, with Air Force One as a dramatic backdrop, President Johnson greets military personnel at Travis Air Force Base, California, in December 1967.

Below, right: On his celebrated around-the-world flight in December 1967, President Johnson made a stop at Korat Air Base, Thailand, where he spoke to the assembled military personnel on his goals for the Vietnam War.

President Johnson, his staff and the press pool in tow, departed Andrews on what became a five-day world tour, flying a total of 28,210 miles. The president met with leaders of fourteen countries. The itinerary included Travis Air Force Base in California; Honolulu; Pago Pago; the Australian cities of Canberra, Melbourne, and Darwin; Korat Air Force Base in Thailand; Cam Ranh Bay, South Vietnam; Karachi, Pakistan; Rome and the Vatican; and the Azores. Exhausted, the presidential party returned to Washington on December 24.

The formal reason for the trip was to attend the funeral of Prime Minister Harold Holt of Australia, who had disappeared while swimming in the shark-infested waters off Melbourne (his body was never found). While in Australia the press corps got one night of rest — in the words of Associated Press reporter Frank Cormier, "our first and our last for some time."[21]

The following days included seemingly endless travel without any knowledge among the press of the itinerary or when the presidential tour would end. This extraordinary lack of detail led to considerable confusion, then outright anger. There were few opportunities for the reporters to file stories. Sleepless nights, primitive accommodations on cots, sudden calls to follow the president to an unscheduled speech, chronic problems in maintaining communications with home, and abrupt announcements for yet another flight to an undisclosed destination — this became the universal experience of the journalists attached to the trip.

Only when the presidential party reached Karachi, Pakistan, did the exhausted reporters learn that they were, in fact, on a flight around the world. Responding to the discontent of the press, presidential aide Jack Valenti called an impromptu conference on the tarmac near Air Force One. Hugh Sidey, *Time* magazine's veteran White House reporter, told the president's trusted aide: "This is a flying circus and you know it and the president knows it. The best damn thing you and the president can do is start up this airplane, turn it around and head back home right now, in the same direction we came from."[22] A sharp exchange followed between the two men. In the words of Valenti, "We surveyed each other like two bottled scorpions."[23] Sidey's outburst did not alter the momentum of the trip, but the president did allow a small number of reporters, including Sidey, to fly the next leg on the more luxurious Air Force One. Until then all reporters had been restricted to a no-frills charter jet airliner.[24]

Images of President Johnson on the Asian leg of his world tour in December 1967. *Below, left:* Johnson meets with Pakistani president Ayub Khan (*on right*) in Karachi. Earlier that day Johnson was in Vietnam, where he spoke to military personnel, *center,* and personally greeted a soldier, *right,* at Cam Ranh Bay.

An Inside Look at Air Force One
A Pictorial Time Capsule of LBJ's "Own Little Plane"

n June 1964, *Look,* a national magazine boasting a circulation of 7,400,000, published an illustrated article on Air Force One. A cover story, "The Flying White House," portrayed Lyndon B. Johnson at the apogee of his power, giving the reader a rare profile of the operational life of Air Force One — or what the president affectionately called his "own little plane."

Readers were well aware that LBJ's presidential jet, SAM 26000, had acquired legendary status in the service of his predecessor, John F. Kennedy, playing a central role in the events surrounding the Kennedy assassination the year before. The scoop by *Look* helped to satisfy popular curiosity about Air Force One.

Look's editors took pains to portray in words and images every critical detail of the presidential aircraft's altered lifestyle under President

Col. James B. Swindal, 46, Presidential pilot, has logged almost 16,000 Air Force flight hours since he left his native Alabama to fly combat in World War II.

LOOK

THE CHRISTIAN WAR AGAINST ANTI-SEMITISM

NOW MORE THAN 7,400,000 CIRCULATION

25 CENTS · JUNE 2, 1964

An exclusive picture story inside the plane that carries the fate of the world

THE FLYING WHITE HOUSE

THE FLYING

Speed, safety, style mark Air Force One when the President flies

In flight, as seen in the picture to the left over the New Jersey coast, Air Force One normally weighs about 110 tons, but the pride of executive transports is sleek, graceful, swift. The President's seal adorns the forward fuselage. In this custom Boeing 707, John F. Kennedy flew 75,682 miles. And it was Air Force One that bore his body back from Dallas on Black Friday.

WHITE HOUSE

When President Johnson is aboard, top safety precautions become automatic. Air Force One, seen below taking off at Palm Springs, Calif., is always followed by fire truck and ambulance on commercial and military runways. At airports, planes do not land or take off for 15 minutes in advance of Air Force One's arrival. In flight, LBJ's plane gets air-lane priority.

continued

Johnson. *Look* provided images of the president with his family, his advisers, and guest congressmen aboard the White House plane. Mirrored in these scenes was the ambience of a busy workplace, where, as the writers described it, "LBJ runs the nation from 30,000 feet." The article offered a rare cameo of the pilot in command, Colonel James Swindal, the former pilot for President Kennedy. His command role was fleshed out with reference to his crew, including a co-pilot, a flight engineer, a navigator, a radioman, and flight attendants, all U.S. Air Force personnel.

The photo essay told of numerous items bearing the presidential seal and the inscription "Air Force Number One" [sic], including pillow cases, blankets, china, playing cards, memo pads, and assorted souvenirs. Readers learned that the Johnson family also traveled with their own insignia, their special luggage with the "LBJ diamond brand."

The plane's interior appointments, always a matter of speculation, were described, including two Air Force One galleys, one forward and one aft, preparing a "typical lunch aloft" of vegetable beef soup, tuna fish sandwiches, decaffeinated coffee, and bottled water. Passengers often relaxed in the large passenger compartment with a cigarette in hand.

Look also revealed that the presidential plane had eight communications channels, six of which could put the president in touch with military bases around the globe. There were oblique references to encryption machines, direct phone links to the White House, and the president's capability while aloft to exercise full control over the vast and lethal war-making power of the U.S. military.

LBJ talks to Senators Smathers (beside Mrs. Johnson) and Holland as Senator Magnuson chats with Lynda Bird.

LBJ runs nation from 30,000 feet

Lyndon B. Johnson takes as naturally to the nation's No. 1 plane as he does to the White House. Flying from Washington to Florida for a mixed bag of politics and ceremonies (and a visit to invalided Joseph P. Kennedy at Palm Beach), Johnson dictated, telephoned and transacted business of state. He also talked politics with the passel of senators and congressmen who accepted his invitation to fly with him aboard the Presidential plane—a cherished invitation that is seldom declined. At odd moments, he roved the huge plane, chatting and joking with newspapermen, White House staffers and crew members.

Representatives Pepper, Kirwan, Fascell get the word aloft.

President Johnson visits newspapermen in rear passenger compartment. His secretary, Juanita Roberts, relaxes.

The President and the First Lady board the Presidential plane as flight steward stands by. Lady Bird once disliked flying, is now neutral. Lyndon Johnson enjoys jet travel.

continued

PHOTOGRAPHED BY STANLEY TRETICK   TEXT BY FLETCHER KNEBEL

These technical systems, cloaked in secrecy, stood in contrast to the ubiquitous ceiling speakers pumping "radio and hi-fi music" into the plane, always at the president's command, when he was not roving about "chatting and joking with newspapermen, White House staffers, and crew members."

Air Force One in the 1960s had achieved a stunning new level of technical sophistication. Presidential travel had never been so swift, comfortable, and awe-inspiring. *Look*'s portrayal of Johnson aloft suggested that Air Force One had become a vital, even essential, part of the executive branch of government. Its photomontage and lively text became a time capsule of Air Force One.[25]

Like the captain of a ship, Colonel Swindal rules his plane day and night.

Any point on the globe can be reached from plane's communications hub.

Were the Cubans planning murder?

Never before in history had a Presidential flight over U.S. territory been so camouflaged by security measures and ruses as that of last February 27. A routine trip to Miami for a Democratic fund-raising dinner was turned into a high-tension flight by an FBI tip that a Cuban pilot might try to demolish the President's plane by ramming or shooting. All of the pictures on these two pages and many of the others were taken during the Florida flight at a time when most of those aboard were unaware of the unusual safeguards in effect. While the Secret Service did not believe that Fidel Castro would be so monstrously foolish as to try to kill President Johnson and his family, the agents could take no chances. They masked the President's trip with all possible means. The Presidential plane, with its telltale seal, was pulled out of service. Instead, the White House party flew in a similar executive transport. A visit to Joseph P. Kennedy was not announced in advance. Instead of landing as scheduled at Miami, the plane stopped off at Palm Beach, then went on south to Homestead Air Force Base, while LBJ and family 'copted to Miami Beach. Air Force fighters flew high cover. Plane markings were painted out. Armed boats patrolled off Miami. Returning to Washington, LBJ left secretly at dawn from Homestead AFB.

Swindal and fellow officers check the Florida weather at Jacksonville Naval Air Station.

Air Force One's crew of 13 inspects plane at every stop. Home ground crew numbers 12.

Johnson runs under escort   from jet to helicopter.

continued

The *Look* magazine cover story offered a unique glimpse inside the president's plane, as well as the political climate of the era. Tensions with Cuba still ran high almost a year and a half after the Cuban Missile Crisis in October 1962. As a result, the normal procedures for Air Force One were suspended for the routine flight to Florida covered in the article. The author noted some of the special measures that were taken: "Three identical Boeing 707s, with the numbers painted out, were over Florida at once to confuse would-be attackers. Unannounced stops and helicopter flights — jet-escorted — were made, and the real presidential plane spent the night at Homestead Air Force Base under heavy guard."

"Now, you fellows know I work as hard on this airplane as I do in the White House — maybe harder." Lyndon B. Johnson

The presidential party pressed on to Rome, landing at Ciampino Airport. The trip to Italy was to fulfill Johnson's wish to meet Pope Paul VI and argue the moral legitimacy of the Vietnam War. A helicopter flight to the Vatican soon followed. In his memoir, LBJ adopted an understated style to describe his night trip by helicopter flight to the Vatican, gushing like a tourist that the "Eternal City is a dazzling sight at night" and that, after his helicopter circled the Vatican, it landed "after careful maneuvering."[26] For others who were on the unprecedented trek to the Vatican, the event was filled with danger and many bizarre moments. Frank Cormier described the episode as "unforgettable." The president's helicopter landed on an open area in a small garden — the first time ever a visitor had arrived in Vatican City by helicopter.[27]

Jack Valenti, who accompanied the president in the lead helicopter, described the descent onto the improvised pad as "a hairy experience, a virgin landing in the dark, putting down on the head of a pin!"[28] It had been a white-knuckle affair, and Valenti realized the dangers the flight had posed for all who visited the Vatican that December night.

When the president's helicopter landed, its wheels sank deep into the mud. This meant that the accompanying press helicopter had to be ordered to circle St. Peter's Basilica for more than a half hour to burn off enough fuel to lighten it for a safe landing. "The massive church," Cormier remembered, "was so close you felt you could reach out the open door and touch it. St. Peter's Square also was illuminated. In less then twenty-four hours it would be Christmas Eve, a circumstance that added to the awe we felt as we circled this great landmark of Christendom."[29]

The meeting of President Johnson and Pope Paul VI was cordial, but it did not lead to any particular benefit for the White House's drive to mobilize worldwide support for the war in Vietnam. The two men exchanged gifts, the

Below: **Pope Paul VI holds a bust of LBJ,** given to him by a smiling President Johnson on a whirlwind visit to the Vatican on Christmas Eve, 1967. *Opposite:* **Daughter Luci Baines Johnson joins President Johnson with the family dog, Him,** in tow, for a flight to Texas on Air Force One in December 1964.

pontiff giving the American president a sixteenth-century painting of the Nativity and receiving in turn a five-inch bronze bust of LBJ, one of many handed out to world leaders on the remarkable presidential journey of 1967.[30] Amidst rumors of a possible presidential visit to Ireland, President Johnson chose to fly home via the Azores, arriving in Washington at 4:18 A.M. on Christmas Eve.

The German periodical *Die Welt* found it irresistible to view the spectacle of the globe-trotting American president in terms of Jules Verne, the author of *Around the World in Eighty Days:* "It was a performance that degraded Jules Verne's hero, who had circled the world in eighty days, to a comic figure. It was a running, extravagant feat that mocked every rule of protocol."[31]

Chapter Four

Fateful Flights

Richard Nixon, Gerald Ford, and Jimmy Carter

Richard Nixon's inauguration in January 1969 coincided with a major event in the history of Air Force One: the decision to refurbish SAM 26000. Just weeks after Nixon took the oath of office, the fabled presidential plane of the Kennedy–Johnson years entered a scheduled program of repairs and upgrades. The process of refurbishing SAM 26000 took three months. While denied immediate access to the historic plane, Nixon found some consolation in the fact that he and his staff were offered a key role in its redesign. White House chief of staff H. R. Haldeman took the lead in reshaping the interior design of SAM 26000. And when the plane was retrieved from the cocoon of Boeing Company's aircraft maintenance facility, the interior layout indeed reflected the new president's persona and style.

The transformation of SAM 26000 proved to be an expensive undertaking, a consequence of the painstaking efforts to upgrade the plane in a thorough fashion. No small technical detail was ignored in the process. The interior of the plane was stripped from the nose section to the tail. All electrical and hydraulic systems were examined, tested, and replaced whenever necessary. Upgrades were made on the flight management system and communications gear, transforming the historic presidential airplane into a true high-tech extension of the White House.

Opposite: **President Nixon enjoys the serenity of his private compartment on Air Force One for reading and other work.**
Above: **President Nixon is pictured in his private compartment for a meeting with his national security adviser, Henry Kissinger. Among Nixon's advisers, Kissinger assumed a dominant role in shaping the president's bold diplomatic initiatives to end the war in Vietnam and to establish relations with Communist China.**

President Nixon brought to the interior redesign of SAM 26000 his own penchant for personal privacy. Nixon did not preserve the open floor plan of the Johnson era, the scheme that had allowed LBJ visual and personal access to the airplane from the cockpit to the tail section. By contrast, Nixon's new scheme called for a special three-room suite for the president and his family, just forward of the wing. Once completed, this special compartment served as a combination office, lounge, and bedroom. The multipurpose Nixon design also fashioned a small sitting room for the first lady, a private lavatory, and closets for storage.

A long aisle on the port side of the presidential suite allowed easy access to other compartments in the forward and aft sections of the plane. The plane's floor plan integrated special compartments for the Secret Service, communications gear, and the galleys. A large compartment, equipped with typing stations and desks, housed the presidential staff. The final two compartments, situated in the rear section, included an eight-seat VIP suite and, finally, a small suite for the press and guards.[1]

SAM 26000 continued to serve as Air Force One until 1972, when a second Boeing 707, SAM 27000, became President Nixon's primary jet transport. However, Nixon often chose to fly in the older SAM 26000 when his family accompanied him, largely because of their preference for

"This great plane that took us to China, to Russia...this great Spirit of '76 has got to be remembered." Richard M. Nixon

the historic airplane. As part of the 89th Airlift Wing, SAM 27000 was reserved exclusively for presidential travel. Both planes bore the distinctive Raymond Loewy livery of blue, white, and silver, which by the 1970s had become the fixed and familiar imagery of presidential aircraft.

Nixon took a keen interest in Air Force One during his presidency, inaugurating a number of changes that reflected his personal infatuation with the symbols of state. Not all his innovations won universal applause or endured. With the Bicentennial of the American Revolution near at hand, he chose to dub SAM 26000 the "Spirit of '76," which he had painted on the nose of the presidential plane. He also approved the design of special Air Force One jackets emblazoned with the presidential seal. For the presidential staff, these jackets became a singular perk during the Nixon years. These changes garnered less public attention or criticism than President Nixon's ill-fated campaign to fit White House security personnel with special uniforms reminiscent of those worn by European palace guards in times past.

White House Chief of Staff Haldeman was often a stickler for details on Air Force One. When *Time* magazine published a photograph of President Nixon conferring with Henry Kissinger in the lounge of Air Force One, Haldeman was angered that the large seal of the president was not in any proximity to the chief executive. Accordingly, he ordered the seal moved to the wall behind the president's chair, to ensure that any future photograph would convey the proper image.[2]

Throughout his years as president, Nixon displayed a genuine passion for travel, making frequent trips to his homes in Florida and California. However, it was Nixon's highly publicized foreign journeys that proved dramatic and memorable, a sequence of flights on Air Force One that expressed the administration's foreign policy priorities. One of them, his extraordinary trip to the People's

On the eve of the American Bicentennial, President Nixon christened Air Force One the "Spirit of '76." He later ordered the same designation for SAM 27000, his primary presidential transport. With the passing of the bicentennial celebrations, the name was eventually removed from the aircraft.

Republic of China, genuinely altered the course of international affairs.

Nixon's trip to Asia took place in July 1969, a thirteen-day itinerary that included stops in the Philippines, Thailand, India, Pakistan, Romania, and Great Britain. That same year, in dramatic fashion, he traveled to a remote sector of the Pacific Ocean to observe the splashdown of the Apollo 11 astronauts after their epic journey to the moon.

Nixon's use of presidential aircraft took a curious and unprecedented turn in his quest to resolve the war in Vietnam. In February 1972, Nixon's globetrotting national security adviser, Henry Kissinger, made a series of clandestine flights on Air Force One. These flights took place against the grim backdrop of the war. The relentless spiral in American casualties had eroded public confidence in the

existing war strategy, giving place to a strong and growing anti-war movement. Nixon himself had taken office with a promise to execute a "secret plan" to end the war in Southeast Asia; nevertheless, the war had persisted. With the approach of the 1972 election year, Nixon and his advisers were keenly interested in reaching a settlement on the Vietnam War, what they called "peace with honor."

The daunting task facing the Nixon administration was to fashion a permanent settlement with the communist North Vietnamese, one that would allow the gradual withdrawal of American troops and a context for the survival of the American-sponsored South Vietnamese government. Nixon's strategy, projected over a three-year period, was to maneuver the North Vietnamese into direct talks with the United States to end the war.

In July 1969, Kissinger had met secretly in Paris with

Above, left: **Kissinger loses himself in thought during a preliminary trip to China on October 26, 1971.** *Right:* **Kissinger made effective use of presidential aircraft for his secret negotiations with the North Vietnamese. He is pictured here shaking hands with Le Duc Tho, the chief negotiator for North Vietnam, in Paris, January 1973.**

Xuan Thuy, a North Vietnamese government official, a meeting that had taken place near Paris during President Nixon's celebrated around-the-world flight. This initial diplomatic encounter set the stage for Kissinger's clandestine flights to Paris in 1972. The process of forging a peace settlement was challenging, and the negotiations between Kissinger and Le Duc Tho, the hard-driving and inflexible North Vietnamese representative, took time and many unexpected turns.

Under a shroud of high secrecy, Kissinger made excellent use of Air Force One to fly to Europe for the talks with Le Duc Tho. The sessions took place outside Paris, where French president Georges Pompidou had offered a secure off-camera locale for the historic negotiations. Nixon had excluded his own State Department and high-ranking Pentagon officials from the process for fear any leak to the

The President Flies Commercial

Nixon Surprises Air Travelers on a DC-IO Flight to Los Angeles

Richard M. Nixon was the only U.S. president ever to fly on a regularly scheduled commercial flight while in office. This flight took place on December 26, 1973, and became one of the most legendary episodes in the history of presidential travel.

On the day chosen for the flight, President Nixon's party of twenty-five people quietly slipped out of the White House and, in a motorcade, made their way to Dulles International Airport in northern Virginia. Successfully evading the White House press corps, Nixon and his entourage flew on United Airlines Flight 55 from Washington to Los Angeles. The whole affair took place under a cloak of secrecy, for security reasons. For the flight on the DC-IO jumbo jet, the president's party purchased thirteen first-class tickets at $217.64 each, and some twelve coach tickets at $167.64 apiece, mostly for the Secret Service agents in tow. In a gesture of personal stewardship, the president insisted on purchasing tickets for himself, First Lady Pat Nixon, and daughter Tricia Nixon Cox. Apparently, no one was bumped on the flight to make room for the president and his large retinue; in fact, Nixon later stated that his choice

of this particular flight was based on the assumption that there would be empty seats and no one would be inconvenienced.

Those who had reserved seats on United Airlines Flight 55 were, to say the least, startled at the fact that the president of the United States had joined them on the transcontinental flight. Nixon abandoned his first-class seat in the forward section of the DC-IO to walk the aisles and to engage in informal conversations with the passengers.

Later, Nixon's deputy communications director, Ken W. Clawson, explained that the unprecedented flight on a commercial airliner was a way for the president "to set an example for the rest of the nation during the current energy crisis." The 1970s had become an era of shortfalls in imported crude oil, rising fuel prices for homes and automo-

Below, left, President Nixon poses with the United pilot and crew. *Above,* Nixon mixes with passengers on a commercial flight from Washington to Los Angeles on December 26, 1973.

biles, and heightened public concern over energy conservation. Nixon's rationale for the flight rested on the assumption that a commercial ticket would cost dramatically less than a similar domestic trip on Air Force One. However, many newspaper editorial responses were highly critical of the Nixon flight, as in the case of the *Washington Post,* where the episode was described as "penny-wise, pound-foolish."[3] Some also asked whether the president had remained in the White House communications net, in case of an emergency. A White House spokesman answered that, yes, President Nixon had remained in touch with government and military nerve centers.[4]

press might compromise the delicate and risky process.[5]

As a ruse, the White House defined the unscheduled flights of Air Force One as training missions, to perfect a less-than-reliable "voice scrambler" system that earlier had been installed in the presidential airplane. Parallel to this deception, Kissinger made effective use of his celebrated reputation as a party-goer to conceal his flights on Air Force One. On the eve of each flight he appeared at a fashionable party in Georgetown on a Friday evening, only to depart directly from the party to Andrews for his whirlwind trip to Europe. Kissinger then used his finite hours in Paris for his discussions with the North Vietnamese. The scenario ended with Kissinger flying home on Air Force One under the strictest secrecy; he then appeared in public in a highly visible fashion, to create the illusion that he had been in town for the entire weekend.

Major General Vernon Walters, the American defense attaché in Paris, made sure the secret flights took place without detection. Walters faced formidable problems in coordinating the flights of Air Force One to various airports in Europe. Mixed with the transatlantic flights were shorter shuttle flights and ground transportation arrangements to assure that Kissinger reached the negotiations without discovery by the press.

Presidential planes were essential to the project. SAM 26000 and the backup VIP plane, SAM 970, provided Kissinger with passage to military fields in Britain and West Germany. The filing of flight plans, often changed en route, required no small amount of ingenuity and coordination. The clever ploy of training flights, executed with the active assistance of the French government, carried the day, allowing Nixon's shadowy diplomacy to go forward. It also provided the crew of Air Force One with a moment of triumph, one achieved outside the parameters of their highly scripted lives. The high-stakes international diplomacy might have inspired a James Bond movie.

Kissinger's shuttle flights to Europe proved successful, setting the stage for a tentative cease-fire in October 1972 and, ultimately, for the complete and final withdrawal of American forces from South Vietnam. Air Force One had been essential to the process. There had been no precedent for the Kissinger flights, but the presidential wing

Below, left: **En route to China, President Nixon confers on Air Force One with Henry Kissinger (*second from left*) and other advisers. Among modern presidents, Nixon is remembered as one of the most frequent flyers on presidential planes for both domestic and foreign travel.**
Right: **President Nixon and First Lady Pat Nixon examine news clippings on their historic trip to China.**

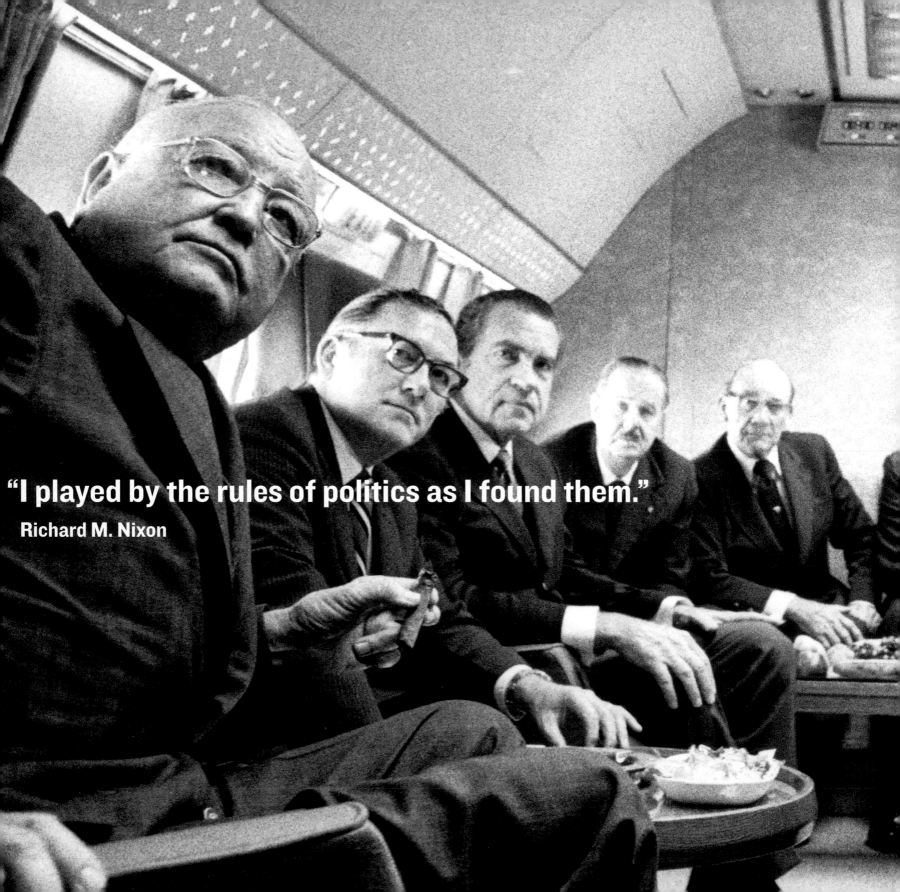

"I played by the rules of politics as I found them."
Richard M. Nixon

President Nixon and a congressional delegation gather on Air Force One to attend the funeral services for Senator Allen J. Ellender in New Orleans on July 31, 1972. Among the dignitaries on the flight are (*from left to right*) Senator James O. Eastland, Senator Robert P. Griffin, President Nixon, Senate Minority Leader Hugh Scott, Senator John McClellan, Senator Milton R. Young, Representative Otto E. Passman, an unidentified politician, Secretary of the Treasury George P. Shultz, and House Majority Leader Hale Boggs.

at Andrews had responded efficiently to the challenge.

Another milestone Nixon established during in his first term in office was the opening of diplomatic relations with communist China. Nixon's flight on Air Force One to China, on February 17, 1972, to engage in direct talks with communist Chinese leader Mao Zedong represented an important and historic breakthrough in the Cold War. In his memoirs, Nixon described his flight to China as "embarking on a voyage of philosophical discovery as uncertain, and in some respects as perilous, as the voyages of geographical discovery of a much earlier time."[6]

The diplomatic breakthrough with China did not come quickly or easily, given the hostility that had characterized Sino-American relations in the years of the Cold War. The communists had assumed power in 1949, but only after a prolonged struggle with the invading Japanese forces in World War II and a brutal internal struggle against the Nationalist Chinese led by Chiang Kai-shek, a longtime ally of the United States.

Like the talks with the North Vietnamese, the preparations for President Nixon's trip to China began clandestinely. While the preparations for the détente with China proceeded on several levels, Kissinger again took the lead in shaping the breakthrough agreement for the historic visit. Kissinger had made a secret trip to China in July 1971, in cooperation with the Pakistani government. The White House worked successfully to keep the press in the dark on the real purpose of Kissinger's Asian trip, given the code name "Polo" after famed explorer Marco Polo. When Kissinger reached Pakistan he met with President Yahya Khan, who in turn invited Nixon's globetrotting adviser to take a brief side trip to his mountain retreat. This feigned interlude for rest allowed Kissinger to make his way to China.

Kissinger had flown to Pakistan in an Air Force C-135, not the well-known SAM 26000 or, for that matter, any

Above: A relaxed President Nixon stands in the aisle of Air Force One on his flight to China. Unlike his predecessor, Lyndon Johnson, Nixon led a cloistered life on the presidential plane, preferring work in his office to socializing.
Right: Bob Haldeman (*center*) held the powerful post of chief of staff under Nixon, and he exerted great influence on Air Force One, from its interior design to the passenger list. Haldeman restricted the press to a rear compartment. Here, he and other White House staff prepare for their meetings with the Chinese.

Scenes from President Richard Nixon's extraordinary journey to China.
Above, left: Workers sweep the streets in anticipation of Nixon's arrival.
Above, second from left: President and Mrs. Nixon disembark from Air Force One upon landing at Beijing.
Above, center: President Nixon shakes hands with Zhou En-lai upon arrival at Beijing.
Above, far right: Nixon and Kissinger meet with the founder of the People's Republic of China, Mao Zedong (at center).
Right: A Chinese honor guard greets the visiting American president at Beijing's international airport.

presidential airplane. For his flight to Beijing from Pakistan, however, he flew on a Pakistani civilian airliner. Kissinger flew to China with a few aides, a contingent of Secret Service agents, and escorts from the Chinese government. Nixon's national security adviser and chief negotiator spent a total of forty-nine hours in China, conferring with Zhou En-lai and other leaders on the details for his boss's visit to the People's Republic. Upon returning to Pakistan, Kissinger sent a one-word message to the White House: "Eureka!" This cryptic message signaled that the proposed presidential visit to China had been approved. On July 15, President Nixon made the dramatic televised announcement of his plans to make a trip to China the following year.

By October 1971, Kissinger was ready to lead an advance party to China to lay the groundwork for the historic encounter of Nixon with Mao Zedong. For this trip, Kissinger flew on SAM 970 with presidential pilot Ralph Albertazzie at the controls. SAM 970 flew the anticipated presidential flight path, stopping at Hawaii and Guam before entering China at Shanghai and then continuing on to Beijing. Kissinger took a contingent of Secret Service agents with him so they could familiarize themselves with airport facilities along the route. For the crew of SAM 970, the Chinese leg of the trip posed real uncertainties. They had no current data on radio frequencies, landing procedures, or protocols for flying in Chinese air space. There were other technical concerns, such as the availability of

"When our hands met, one era ended and another began."

Richard Nixon, on meeting Chinese premier Zhou En-lai

compatible linkage to auxiliary ground power, among myriad other problems. Independently, Colonel Albertazzie obtained classified high-altitude photographs of Chinese airports taken by American SR-71 surveillance aircraft.

The more Nixon's pilot examined the nature of Chinese airport facilities, the more he became concerned about the primitive nature of Chinese commercial aviation. However, there was reassuring news from Pakistani commercial pilots who flew regularly into Shanghai, who reported that landing procedures were identical to those found in the West. Despite all the ambiguities, the exploratory trip to China went well. For the crew, there were interludes for tourism, banquets, and interesting encounters with Chinese aviation personnel.[7]

All these preparations came to fruition on a cold February morning when Air Force One landed at Beijing's airport. As President Nixon disembarked, he was greeted by Zhou En-lai and an honor guard, backed up by a band playing "The Star-Spangled Banner." The ceremony took place in the shadow of the airport's buildings festooned with red banners emblazoned with the slogans "Long Live

Top: Nixon holds a conference with Western press members during his trip to China.
Above: President Richard Nixon and First Lady Pat Nixon visit the Great Wall of China and the Ming tombs, February 1972.

the Chinese Communist Party" and "Long Live the Great Solidarity of All the World's People."

Television cameras conveyed the historic landing of Air Force One around the world. Five hours later President Nixon met with Mao Zedong, a memorable conclave that ended a generation of open hostility in Sino-American relations. Throughout the Chinese trip Air Force One remained parked at the airport, surrounded by guards of both countries, a symbol of the American presidency.[8]

In his memoirs, President Nixon observed that the Chinese, following their own instincts for secrecy, insisted that the presidential airplane fly from Shanghai to Beijing at a low altitude. The flight path gave Nixon a rare opportunity to gaze out the window of Air Force One and see the unfolding Chinese countryside below: "The small towns and villages looked like pictures I had seen of towns in the middle ages." Upon landing in Beijing, the president greeted a hatless Zhou En-lai on the wind-swept ramp of the airport, a man who stood in the cold in a heavy overcoat that "did not hide the thinness of his frail body." Nixon knew that Zhou En-lai had been snubbed at the Geneva conference in 1954, when American secretary of state John Foster Dulles had refused to shake his hand: "Therefore, I made a point of extending my hand as I walked toward him. When our hands met, one era ended and another began."[9]

Life on Nixon's Air Force One, the famed reporter Theodore White once noted, invited little conviviality. White observed that President Nixon had brought to presidential travel a "compulsive wish for privacy." Air Force One indeed mirrored the personality of this president in charge. When the extrovert Lyndon Johnson roamed freely throughout the plane, those on board — crew, staff, VIPs, reporters — all were in constant visual contact with the chief executive. By contrast, Nixon preferred the isolation of his private compartment, rarely wandering about or visiting the cockpit area. In the words of White, he was "invisible," working in his presidential "lair," alone at his tiny desk. President Nixon's hierarchical style, which bequeathed to the grim and demanding chief of staff H. R. Haldeman complete control, did not permit a mood of lightheartedness or spontaneity on Air Force One. Not only was Nixon out of sight, White observed, but "no one ventured forward from the rear of the plane to staff territory without permission; and no one on the staff, except Haldeman and Ziegler [Nixon's press secretary], ventured forth from the staff territory to the President's territory without being asked."[10]

Nixon won reelection in 1972 in a record landslide. Now at the apogee of his power and influence, the president ironically found himself caught up in the Watergate crisis, a political disaster of his own making. This scandal eventually cast Nixon from the exalted heights of presidential power to the uncharted domain of forced resignation.

The "Watergate affair" referred narrowly to the break-in and electronic bugging in 1972 of the Democratic National Committee headquarters in the Watergate apartment and office complex in Washington, D.C. The unfolding scandal involved no less than thirty Nixon administration officials, campaign officials, and financial contributors pleading guilty or being found guilty of breaking the law. In the aftermath of the event, Nixon's White House sought unsuccessfully to shield the president's own knowledge of the affair and efforts toward a cover-up. The whole scandal raised constitutional questions and prompted a majority in the House Judiciary Committee to favor a vote for impeachment. Facing this inevitability, Nixon resigned on August 9, 1974. Gerald Ford, his vice president, assumed the office of the presidency for the remainder of Nixon's term.

Air Force One played a highly visible role in the climactic hours of Nixon's presidency. The symbolic final moment came over Missouri en route to California, when Colonel Albertazzie — taking note of the exact time of Gerald Ford's swearing in at the White House — requested air traffic control in the Kansas City Center to change the airplane's call sign from Air Force One to simply SAM 26000. In an instant, the immense power of the American presidency had passed from one man to another. The airplane continued on its flight path to California, no longer Air Force One, but still a symbol of the American presidency.

Gerald R. Ford

When Gerald Ford took the oath of office, he remarked with some understatement that he had assumed the highest office of the land "under extraordinary circumstances." He brought a reputation for personal integrity to the White House and spent considerable energy fashioning a new sense of national unity in the aftermath of the Watergate scandal. Ford had spent a total of twenty-five years as a

Below: **Gerald and Betty Ford walk away from Marine One on the White House Lawn on President Nixon's last day in office. Later in the day, Richard and Pat Nixon wave to onlookers,** *bottom,* **after their final flight to California on board Air Force One.**

Air Force One in the "Final Days"
As the Watergate Scandal Deepens, Nixon Flees to the Middle East

The saga of Richard Nixon's final weeks as president of the United States remains one of the most dramatic episodes in American history. In the summer of 1974, as the Watergate crisis reached critical mass, Nixon decided impulsively to travel on Air Force One to Europe and the Middle East, an eleventh-hour gesture aimed at shoring up his reputation. The extraordinary trip proved to be a hazardous undertaking for the embattled president, done at great risk to his personal health and in the face of unforeseen dangers.

On June 12, after a stopover in Salzburg, Austria, President Nixon flew to Cairo, Egypt, to launch his tour of the Middle East. His decision to fly to Cairo ran counter to the anxious pleadings of one of his doctors, Walter Tkach. Dr. Tkach had diagnosed Nixon's swollen left leg as a telltale sign of phlebitis, a potentially life-threatening condition: a blood clot in the president's leg could break loose and move quickly to either the heart or lungs, leading to instant death. The itinerary was ambitious, and in the course of his visit to the Egyptian cities of Cairo and Alexandria, Nixon would be called upon to stand for extended periods of time, to climb stairs, and to move about on foot repeatedly — the very sort of movement that would aggravate his condition. The president rejected the advice of Tkach and others who urged caution, stating that the "trip is more important than my life, I know it is a calculated risk."[1] As events unfolded, many wondered if Nixon, in fact, had actually demonstrated a death wish.

The trip to Egypt proved to be a whirlwind tour, one where cheering crowds came out in enormous numbers to greet Nixon and his host, President Anwar el-Sadat. On the railroad trip to Alexandria, in particular, the enthusiasm of the Egyptian crowds reached fever pitch: workers, peasants, soldiers, and schoolchildren lined both sides of the track shouting their approval of the visiting American president and waving "We trust Nixon" banners. However, the Secret Service escorts grew increasingly alarmed about the vulnerability of the president to a terrorist attack, especially on the final motorcade to the Cairo airport, when Nixon left his limousine to wade into the crowd of cheering onlookers.

After a short stopover in Saudi Arabia, Nixon flew to Damascus, Syria, on June 15. Flying to Damascus ran counter to the advice of some of his advisers, who had urged the cancellation of this part of the itinerary, arguing that forces hostile to the United States might attempt an act of terror against the presidential party. Nixon ignored their pleas.

The flight to Damascus brought unexpected dangers: four Syrian MiGs entered the flight path of Air Force One. The Syrian jets appeared just as the president's pilot, Colonel Ralph Albertazzie, made his descent into Damascus, roughly at fifteen thousand feet. No foreign fighter escorts had been approved for Air Force One, so this untoward event prompted considerable alarm on board the presidential plane. Colonel Albertazzie took no chances, putting Air Force One into a series of evasive maneuvers, banks, and turns for several minutes. Finally, as the Syrian jets remained close and posed no apparent threat, Albertazzie resumed his approach into Damascus.

Henry Kissinger, in his memoirs, recorded that many on Air Force One were visibly shaken by the experience, fearing that Syrians or some rogue terrorist group planned to attack the presidential plane. Had Nixon placed himself and his party in harm's way? Kissinger observed, "Never was an

Opposite: President Nixon waves to an Egyptian crowd as he travels by rail from Cairo to Alexandria. Egyptian president Anwar el-Sadat is partially visible at left.

Right: President Nixon departs with his family from the White House on his last day in office. Gerald Ford, soon to be sworn in as president, bids Nixon farewell.

Below: President Nixon makes his final salute as he departs on Marine One for Andrews Air Force Base, to board Air Force One for his flight to California.

American delegation happier to reach Damascus than on this occasion."[12]

Nixon returned to Washington only to discover that the Watergate crisis now loomed as an even greater threat to his presidency, with the dramatic loss of popular support and Congress moving irreversibly toward a bill of impeachment. Faced with these grim circumstances, Nixon opted to resign from office, effective at noon on August 9, 1974.

Nixon later recorded in his memoirs his recollections of that fateful day: "The memory of that scene for me is like a frame forever frozen at that moment: the red carpet, the green lawn, the white house, the leaden sky. . . . I raised my arms in a final salute. I smiled. I waved goodbye. I turned into the helicopter, the door was closed, the red carpet was rolled up. The engines started. The blades began to turn. The noise grew until it almost blotted out thought. Suddenly, slowly we began to rise. The people on the ground were waving. The White House was behind us now. . . . There was no talk. There were no tears left. I leaned my head back against the seat and closed my eyes. I heard Pat saying to no one in particular, 'It is so sad. It is so sad.' Another swing and we were on course for Andrews, where Air Force One was waiting for the flight home to California."[13]

Nixon's final hours as chief executive were spent aloft on the presidential plane, with the historic passage from president to private citizen marked in time — in the skies over Missouri — by Gerald Ford taking the oath of office as president of the United States.

Left: President Gerald Ford confers with his secretary of state, Henry Kissinger, on Air Force One en route to Vladivostok to meet Soviet leader Leonid Brezhnev, November 1974.

Below: President Ford enjoys a jovial moment with his host, Leonid Brezhnev, at Vladivostok in the Soviet Far East, November 23, 1974. Brezhnev, to the amusement of the American delegation, is wearing Ford's parka.

Michigan congressman, with a stint in the powerful post of minority leader in the House of Representatives. For many Americans, the new president's understated style and personal honesty fit the national mood in the summer of 1974, one that desired the occupant of the White House to project an image of normalcy.

An internationalist in foreign affairs, President Ford made effective use of Air Force One for diplomatic missions abroad. In November 1974, Ford flew to Vladivostok to meet with Soviet leader Leonid Brezhnev. Their conclave took place in a health resort in Vladivostok, the Soviet Union's main port on the Pacific Ocean. The session gave full expression to Ford's priority of détente with America's Cold War adversary. Both countries continued to advance the agenda of the SALT II negotiations, which called for limitations on intercontinental ballistic missiles, multiple warheads, and other strategic nuclear weapons.

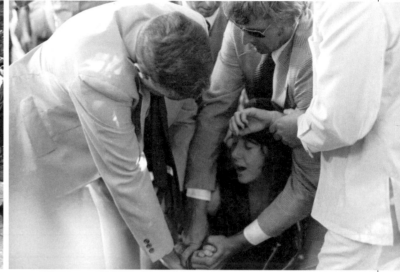

At home, Ford made extensive use of Air Force One to promote his domestic programs. On a seemingly routine trip to Sacramento, California, in September 1975, Ford encountered a potential assassin. The president described in his memoirs the event, which unfolded on the morning of September 5 as he made his way to meet Governor Jerry Brown: "The weather that morning was clear, the sun was shining brightly, and there were several rows of people standing behind a rope that lined the sidewalk on my left. They were applauding. . . . I was in a good mood, so I started shaking hands. That's when I spotted a woman wearing a bright red dress. She was in the second or third row, moving right along with me as if she wanted to shake my hand. When I slowed down, I noticed immediately that she thrust her hand under the arms of the other spectators. I reached down to shake it — and looked into the barrel of a .45 caliber pistol pointed directly at me."[14]

Facing the gun held by the woman in red, President Ford observed that he instinctively "ducked," even as a Secret Service agent wrestled the would-be assassin to the ground. Bystanders reported the woman yelled, "This country is a mess. This man is not your president."[15] Later

Left: Secret Service agents and police rush to protect President Ford in the aftermath of the assassination attempt by Lynette "Squeaky" Fromme, September 5, 1975.
Right: Secret Service agents subdue and hand-cuff Fromme.
Above: Fromme, dressed in red, leaving the court-house in Sacramento after her first hearing on the attempt to assassi-nate President Ford.

it was learned that she was Lynette "Squeaky" Fromme, an erstwhile follower of Charles Manson and an activist in the environmental movement. She wore her "ceremonial red dress" whenever she went about "cleaning the earth."

In the face of this incident, President Ford displayed considerable coolness, keeping his appointment with Governor Brown and adhering to the scheduled itinerary. On the return flight to Washington, Ford displayed little emotion in the aftermath of his narrow escape from death, seeming relaxed as he smoked his pipe and joked with reporters.

Having dodged one violent assault on his life, President Ford encountered yet another assassination attempt only seventeen days later. After addressing a luncheon meeting with the AFL–CIO building and construction trades unions in San Francisco, Ford walked toward his limousine only to hear a gun fire: "Bang! I recognized the sound of the shot, and I froze. There was a hushed silence for a split second. Then pandemonium broke out."[16] Two Secret Service agents rushed to the president, forcing him down and then into the limousine. The agents and presidential aides piled on Ford to shield him from any harm; agents

pinned the president to the floor for the fast ride back to the airport, one the chief executive found uncomfortable, leaving him little room to breathe.

For the beleaguered president, Air Force One again provided a secure refuge. Upon reaching the presidential plane there was an unanticipated moment of humor, when a smiling David Kennerly, the White House photographer, greeted Ford with the question, "Other than that, Mr. President, how did you like San Francisco?"[17] Kennerly's query prompted a grin from Ford, who later observed that this question had broken the tension and allowed everyone to regain some sense of tranquility. First Lady Betty Ford, on a side trip to Monterey and not knowing of the assassination attempt, unwittingly added to the humor of the occasion when she entered the cabin of Air Force One, asking her husband: "Well, how did they treat you in San Francisco?"[18]

The woman seeking to assassinate Ford that day was Sara Jane Moore. She had fired a shot from a .38-caliber Smith and Wesson revolver. Moore's shot missed President Ford by five feet, ricocheted off a wall, and wounded a cab driver. An alert bystander, Oliver Sipple, had grabbed

Left: President Ford waves to the crowd outside the St. Francis Hotel in San Francisco on September 22, 1975, moments before being shot at by Sara Jane Moore.
Center: The president winces at the sound of the gunshots fired by Moore.
Right: Ford ducks, as Secret Service agents hustle him into a waiting limousine. He was rushed to Air Force One.
Above: Moore in custody after her attempt to assassinate the president.

Moore's arm as soon as he saw the revolver, causing her to miss her intended target. After her arrest, Moore stated that her purpose was to unite the Bay Area radicals, as expressed in her poem, "let my gun sing for the people. / Scream their anger, cleanse with their / hate, / and kill this monster."[19] At the age of forty-five, Moore had been a one-time FBI informant on the kidnapping of Patty Hearst and a habitué in the counterculture movement in San Francisco. Both Moore and Fromme received life sentences for their separate attempts on the life of President Ford.

On the flight home on Air Force One, President Ford, with a martini in hand, again remained calm and reassuring, although the Secret Service and the president's advisers were deeply troubled by the two assassination attempts in California. "I was determined," Ford later wrote, "not to let the second near miss intimidate me, and when we returned to the White House later that night, I told reporters: 'I don't think any person as president ought to cower in the face of a limited number of people who want to take the law into their own hands.' And if we can't have that opportunity of talking with one another, seeing one another, shaking hands with one another, something has

"I am a Ford, not a Lincoln." Gerald R. Ford

gone wrong in our society."[20] At the insistence of the Secret Service, however, Ford agreed to wear a bulletproof vest. In the aftermath of the abortive assassinations, Congress quickly funded the hiring of 150 new Secret Service agents, among other steps to assure adequate protection for the president and presidential candidates in the coming 1976 election.

The 1970s were also a time of airline hijackings, most often to Castro's Cuba, and the growing threat of global terrorism. Such lawless behavior stood as a powerful challenge to national security. Under a shroud of secrecy, the U.S. Air Force took steps to enhance the safety of Air Force One, equipping both VC-137Cs with an infrared countermeasures self-defense system to protect against heat-seeking missiles. Fears of a rogue attack by a terrorist with a shoulder-mounted, heat-seeking missile prompted this and other moves to assure the safety of a traveling president.[21]

President Ford lost his bid for reelection in 1976 to the Democratic candidate, Governor Jimmy Carter of Georgia. Ford's tenure in office had been short, too short to establish any dramatic change in the operation of Air Force One.

Jimmy Carter

James Earl Carter Jr., known popularly as Jimmy Carter, came to the White House out of relative obscurity. In the immediate aftermath of the Watergate years, Carter represented to many Americans a person of high purpose and moral integrity. His administration would be credited with a major diplomatic breakthrough in the quest for a Middle East settlement, the Camp David accords between Israel and Egypt, but Carter's inability to contend effectively with pressing domestic and foreign policy challenges would deny him reelection in 1980.

As president, Carter made some dramatic changes to White House travel, representing a shift in style that expressed his own personal values. He preferred simplicity and informality in all his travels, and Air Force One changed accordingly. Carter's innovations proved to be temporary, but they echoed the older debate on presidential travel going back to the nineteenth century: should a president, by virtue of the Constitution a citizen with only a temporary mandate to exercise executive power, be transported in monarchical trappings? The 1970s had given birth to a debate on the "Imperial Presidency," and Carter represented one antidote to this perceived corruption of democratic values.

Taking office on January 20, 1977, President Carter quickly revealed his new stress on informality, rejecting a limousine to walk down Pennsylvania Avenue to the White House following his inaugural address. On the ground, he preferred an armored Ford LTD sedan to the luxurious Lincoln limousines used by his predecessors.

Opposite: President Ford displayed considerable serenity in the face of two attempts on his life. Here he relaxes with his wife, Betty, on their return flight to Washington from San Francisco after the second assassination attempt.
Below: President Carter waves to a crowd of supporters before boarding Air Force One on May 17, 1977. He was known for bringing simplicity and austerity to White House air travel operations.

Fateful Flights **117**

Fellow Travelers
The Press Corps Finds Time to Play Poker and Eat Good Food

Presidential travel has long included representatives from the press, a practice that can be traced back at least to Abraham Lincoln. As president-elect, Lincoln set aside a special railway car for the press corps to accompany him on his journey from Springfield, Illinois, to Washington, D.C., in 1861. Since then, the press has been the constant companion of presidents on their domestic and foreign journeys. At times, presidents have warmly embraced the Fourth Estate; on other occasions, the White House posture toward reporters has been one of thinly veiled hostility.

A press pool—a small group of reporters representing the entire press corps — for Air Force One became formalized in the 1960s. These pool reporters were assigned to the small press compartment on Air Force One. Pool members listened to press briefings, queried the president's press secretary and staff for news, and then prepared a report to be disseminated among their fellow professional journalists on the press charters. More often than not, flying on Air Force One did not afford any opportunity to meet and talk with the president. Only highly gregarious presidents such as Gerald Ford and Bill Clinton frequently sought out the press pool reporters for conversation.

Initially, the number of reporters admitted to the pool was small, typically four people — two reporters from the wire services, a representative from one of the three major television networks, and a fourth journalist from a major magazine or perhaps the local newspaper of the town the president planned to visit. Later, the press pool was enlarged to include as many as twelve to fourteen reporters, a change explained in part by the enlarging scope of presidential travel and the advent of cable-television news with its twenty-four-hour coverage.

Those in the large press contingent not assigned to Air Force One typically fly on one or two chartered planes. The White House Travel Office plans these special flights, arranging for ground transportation, hotel reservations, and the press center upon landing. In the 1960s and 1970s, Pan Am and TWA vied to win the bid for the overseas press charters. They competed by offering upscale accommodations for the press and White House personnel who flew on the charters.

Flying on a press charter, as former CBS reporter Robert Pierpoint remembered, was "a time to play poker and eat good food." Pierpoint's CBS colleague Bob Schieffer also observed that a party ambience prevailed on many press charter flights. The airlines typically prepared gourmet menus and, on occasion, called upon the flight attendants to dress up in special costumes. In the words of one reporter, Eleanor Randolph, the press planes appeared to be loaded with "more liquor than fuel." Yet such flights were tame enough for families; Pierpoint remembers taking his wife and children on a press charter to California during the Nixon years.[22]

Flying with a president on Air Force One could provide rare occasions to see the chief executive act in a spontaneous way. Pierpoint observed Richard Nixon on his first overseas trip to meet French president Charles de Gaulle. Upon landing at Orly Airport, Nixon spotted de Gaulle standing

During an Air Force One flight on November 7, 1972, longtime presidential photographer Ollie Atkins seizes the opportunity to take a photograph of Henry Kissinger.

"There is no travel like traveling with the president."
Bob Schieffer

with his honor guard in the rain without an over-coat; the American president tossed his overcoat aside and departed Air Force One with the comment to the reporters, "Vive la France!"

There were excruciating times as well, as when Pierpoint and his press colleagues were forced to listen to a defense of the Vietnam War by Lyndon Johnson, a two-hour lecture delivered from his "throne chair" while on a trip to Texas on Air Force One. Flying to Plains, Georgia, as Pierpoint recollected, always meant spartan accommodations for the press in a motel located in a nearby town. On Sundays, the Secret Service denied the press access to Jimmy Carter's church, which meant an entire morning standing outside in the hot sun as the president attended Sunday school and the worship service.

As the members of the press pool well know, traveling with the president comes with as many challenges as opportunities.

Scenes of the press pool on board Air Force One. President Nixon, *top left,* makes a rare appearance to talk with reporters on December 12, 1970. President George H. W. Bush, *top right,* talks to reporters, including longtime White House correspondent Helen Thomas, who stands beside him. A triumphant President Clinton, *middle row left,* talks to reporters about his 1996 reelection campaign the day after he defeated Republican candidate Bob Dole. Advisor George Stephanopoulos is at right, and Clinton's chief of staff, Leon Panetta, is behind them. Reporters on the press charter, *middle row right,* arrange an improvised "happy hour" on a flight from Ottawa to Chicago in October 1999. White House photographer David Kennerly (*on left*) and Chief of Protocol Henry Catto, *bottom,* play cards on a trip to the Far East in November 1974. Journalists on Air Force One on May 17, 1999, *opposite,* reenact the impact of heavy turbulence they encountered on the previous day.

Left: President Carter signals his informal style during his inauguration as he walks from the Capitol to the White House after taking the oath of office. *Above:* Amy Carter steps from Air Force One to join her parents for the short shuttle flight on Marine One from Andrews Air Force Base to the White House, circa April 1979.

His most dramatic gesture was to insist that he and members of his family carry their own luggage on any trip. Carter made his personal style known on Air Force One, and his no-frills approach represented a dramatic departure from the past. He insisted that Air Force One be a workplace, not an airborne palace; his new rules precluded any of the luxurious trappings that traditionally came with presidential air travel.

Over time, many perks had become available to those who flew on Air Force One, including a variety of souvenirs and gifts emblazoned with the presidential seal for those with the rare privilege to ride on the fabled airplane. President Carter eliminated most of these souvenirs, arguing that they were an unjustified waste of the taxpayers' money.

To make Air Force One operations less ostentatious, Carter called for the elimination of the prefix "V" (the designation for VIPs) from the VC-137C aircraft, which

subsequently flew under the designation "C-137C." Such austerity also extended to the White House and Camp David. Carter brought to his domestic and international air travel a certain — even studied — simplicity. Most of Carter's critics did not challenge his personal sincerity, but many found some of his changes to be petty and misguided, a manifestation of the president's legendary penchant to micromanage the smallest details of White House life. In the end, Carter's campaign for austerity would prove short-lived.

Less apparent at the time was the fact that President Carter actually enjoyed traveling on Air Force One. In fact, he found ways to make effective use of the plane for his political ends, a practice his successors later copied, offering rides on the presidential airplane as a reward or an inducement to support his administration's programs. Even with the spartan ethos of the Carter years, Air Force One retained its allure for all travelers.

President Jimmy Carter enjoys a relaxed moment with Hamilton Jordan and other White House staff on Air Force One, on July 20, 1977.

President Carter in his four years in the White House made regular use of Air Force One for domestic and foreign travel, but no epic journey marked his tenure in office. In early 1979, however, there was one trip that did capture the attention of the nation. An accident at the Three Mile Island nuclear plant near Harrisburg, Pennsylvania, sparked widespread concern about the hazards of nuclear power. Fears abounded that the whole area around Harrisburg might have to be evacuated in the face of the emergency. At the time of the reactor accident, President Carter was in Wisconsin. Carter felt the need to act in some dramatic way to provide reassurance to the country that the problem was under control.

Flying back to Washington on Air Force One, President Carter decided to visit the nuclear reactor and ordered his staff to make arrangements. Carter decided not to take Air Force One on this short hop to Pennsylvania. Instead, he made a one-hour flight on Marine One, the presidential helicopter, landing at an Air National Guard facility in Middletown, three miles upwind from the nuclear reactor site. When the president visited Three Mile Island with First Lady Rosalynn Carter, Pennsylvania governor Richard Thornburgh, and other dignitaries, he donned yellow plastic shoe covers (to prevent tracking any radioactive material on the ground) for his thirty-six-minute tour of the nuclear plant. Later, President Carter gave a short speech, which did much to reassure the nation.

1980 was a difficult year for President Carter, with Iran holding scores of American hostages and the Cold War at its height, the Soviet Union having invaded Afghanistan the year before. The mood of the nation was a somber one, reflecting a severe economic crisis, inflation, and soaring gasoline prices. At Lake Placid, New York, the United States Olympic Hockey team, to the surprise of the world, won the gold medal by defeating the Soviet hockey team, an event that added a moment of uplift in an otherwise grim year. President Carter sent Air Force One to pick up the victorious American hockey squad and bring them to Washington for a special ceremony. For the American hockey Olympians, Air Force One became a magic carpet carrying them to a special White House fete in honor of their improbable victory.

President Carter's most memorable trip on Air Force One actually came after he had left office, in January 1981. The Iranian government, as a final insult to Carter, had waited to release their American hostages until Ronald Reagan had been sworn into office. The new president, however, reacted to this calculated insult by inviting former president Carter to fly on Air Force One to Germany to greet the hostages on behalf of the American people.

While en route to Frankfurt, Germany, where the former hostages had been taken for medical checkups, Carter and his aides were concerned about how they would be received. Their captors in Iran had told them falsely of President Carter's indifference to their fate. Bruce Laingen, the senior American hostage, introduced Carter to the assembled group. The meeting began awkwardly with tentative handshakes, but soon the atmosphere became more upbeat and friendly. The former chief executive later recalled that this reception was one of the most emotional moments in his life.

On the return flight home on Reagan's Air Force One, Hamilton Jordan, Carter's presidential aide, stated that a festive atmosphere pervaded the airplane: "After a big dinner, the President joined a boisterous group that had gathered in the lounge area, and for several hours we swapped stories and exchanged toasts. Most of us had slept only four or five hours in the last two or three days and were operating on adrenaline and champagne."[23]

Above: President Jimmy Carter meets with House Speaker Thomas O'Neill on Air Force One, December 8, 1978.
Right: President Carter meets with his team of advisers on Air Force One during a May 1977 trip to Europe for a G7 economic summit. From left to right are Zbigniew Brzezinski, Michael Blumenthal, Carter, and Cyrus Vance.

Cold War's End

Ronald Reagan and George H. W. Bush

THE ELECTION OF RONALD REAGAN in 1980 signaled a dramatic shift in American foreign policy. The new president set into motion a bold series of initiatives that profoundly altered the tone and course of international affairs. For Reagan, Air Force One became an indispensable vehicle for reaching distant parts of the globe to pursue his ambitious diplomatic goals. His active participation in summitry, in particular with Soviet leader Mikhail Gorbachev, set the stage for the end of the Cold War.

President Reagan's travels on Air Force One began in earnest in his second year in office, after his domestic agenda had been firmly established. Over the next seven years, Reagan became a frequent flyer on the presidential plane, making six pivotal journeys to Europe and three to Asia, along with another twelve trips to America's neighbors in the Western Hemisphere. Reagan's memorable encounters with Gorbachev involved high-stakes negotiations in the shifting locales of Geneva, Reykjavik, and Moscow.[1] Reagan advocated "peace through strength," a formulation of American foreign policy that mirrored his own personal idealism and confidence in the intrinsic strength of the American political system. His ascent to power coincided with a difficult moment in the Cold War, when tension had been heightened by the Soviet invasion of Afghanistan in late 1979. For many, Reagan's posture in

Opposite: **President Reagan waves as he boards Air Force One at Dothan, Alabama, on July 10, 1986. The presidential seal, clearly visible on the open aircraft door, signifies the military power of the presidency.**
Above: **President Reagan (*center*) enjoys a light moment with his staff on Air Force One, April 27, 1983.**

world affairs appeared very risky and at odds with the traditional policy of containment of communism worldwide, first articulated by President Harry S. Truman in the immediate aftermath of World War II. Reagan affirmed that the fortunes of communism indeed could be reversed, perhaps leading to the actual collapse of the political movement itself. Such ideas were novel and, for some, implausible.

Lou Cannon, a newspaper reporter, viewed Reagan as an "embodiment of the American idealism."[2] Whatever his core motives, Reagan brought a personal dynamism and relentless opposition to the status quo in international affairs. He supported labor union activist and reformer Lech Walesa and his Solidarity movement in Poland, actively opposed communist-supported movements in the Western Hemisphere, and gave aid to the Afghan rebels in their struggle against the Soviet invasion of their country.

As president, Reagan displayed great impatience with the notion that détente required passivity toward the Soviet Union or discreet silence on the manifest virtues of democracy over communism. One of his most provocative gestures came in 1983, when he decided to deploy cruise and Pershing missiles in Europe — a move warmly endorsed by British prime minister Margaret Thatcher, French president François Mitterand, and German

On a trip to California on Air Force One, June 29, 1981, President Reagan meets with adviser Richard Allen (*far left*) and members of his staff. Reagan's primary concern in his first year in office was the implementation of his domestic policy, but this priority soon gave way to bold initiatives in foreign policy.

chancellor Helmut Kohl. Reagan's supporters were quick to point out that the deployment of Pershings had been in direct response to the placement of Soviet SS-20 missiles in Eastern Europe. Even more alarming to the Soviet Union was Reagan's decision, announced that same year, to pursue the hotly debated Strategic Defense Initiative (SDI), which called for the use of laser beams and other space-based high technology to provide a shield against ballistic missile attacks on the United States and its allies.

Over time, and in particular after his reelection in 1984, President Reagan shifted from confrontation to negotiation. His ultimate success in the sphere of international diplomacy related, in part, to Gorbachev, his opposite number in the Cold War equation. Gorbachev, the son of peasants and a specialist in agricultural issues, assumed power in the Soviet Union in March 1985. Energetic and youthful, he dramatically pushed his country toward reform, reordering life in the Soviet Union with his programs of *glasnost* (openness) and *perestroika* (restructuring). The new Soviet leader required an accommodation with the West to achieve his pressing political reforms. No less a concern for Gorbachev was the high cost of the Cold War, which required enormous expenditures that otherwise could have been allocated for domestic projects.

Throughout his tenure Reagan routinely flew on SAM 27000, which became the backdrop for all of the president's wide-ranging diplomatic journeys. Air Force One took Reagan to Geneva for his first summit with Gorbachev in November 1985. Reagan, seventy-four, and Gorbachev, fifty-four, met at a lakeside chateau for their first encounter, which proved quite successful in establishing mutual respect and cordiality. Later, the president flew on Air Force One to meet with his Soviet counterpart in a sequence of pivotal meetings in Reykjavik and Moscow. In all these diplomatic contacts with the Russians, Reagan

The History of Tail Number 27000

The Presidential Plane That Transformed International Diplomacy Retires

The Ronald Reagan Presidential Library and Museum in Ventura County, California, plans a special exhibition devoted to presidential travel and Air Force One. Located on a stunning hilltop in the Simi Valley, the Reagan Library will ultimately be the home for SAM 27000.

The plane completed its final positioning flight to San Bernardino International Airport in September 2001 for disassembly and removal to the presidential library. Plans call for SAM 27000 to go on permanent display in late 2004. As Air Force One, the plane flew 444 missions, with more than 211 missions for President Reagan alone. As such, SAM 27000 will forever be associated with the climactic years of the Cold War.

The story of SAM 27000, however, goes back to 1972, when it joined the 89th Airlift Wing at Andrews Air Force Base. As a new Boeing 707 devoted to the exclusive use of the White House, the plane eventually superseded SAM 26000 as the primary Air Force One; where SAM 26000 had become the familiar image of Air Force One under presidents Kennedy and Johnson, SAM 27000 assumed that role in the 1980s under Reagan.

Richard Nixon was the first chief executive to make extensive use of SAM 27000. The life of SAM 27000, extended to 2001, serving no fewer than seven presidents: Richard Nixon, Gerald Ford, Jimmy Carter, Ronald Reagan, George H. W. Bush, Bill Clinton, and George W. Bush. Following the delivery of the new generation of Boeing 747-200B jumbo jets in 1990 and 1991, SAM 27000 was relegated largely to a back-up role, carrying the president only occasionally.

One of most historic moments associated with SAM 27000 took place on August 9, 1974, when the plane flew Richard Nixon home to California after his resignation. While en route, at the moment Nixon's successor, Gerald R. Ford, took the oath of office, the pilot of Air Force One radioed Kansas City Air Traffic Control: "Kansas

Below: President George W. Bush and First Lady Laura Bush relax on board SAM 27000 during its final official flight on August 29, 2001. *Bottom:* The 707, dismantled for transport, rests in a hangar in June 2003 before being transported to the Ronald Reagan Presidential Library, where it will be on permanent display in a special pavilion. *Opposite:* Scenes of tail number 27000 during its long service, from Nixon's 1974 trip to Israel, *upper left,* to Reagan's 1988 visit to Russia, bottom. Captain Ralph Albertazzie and crew, *upper right,* prepare for a flight in China in February 1972.

City, this is Air Force One, please change our call sign to SAM 27000." At that moment, SAM 27000 served as the final and symbolic means to record the transfer of presidential power.

Among all the presidents who flew on SAM 27000, Reagan used it most often. He flew on the aircraft several times during his second term to engage in diplomatic negotiations with Soviet leader Mikhail Gorbachev, at widely separated locales: New York, Reykjavik, and Moscow. The plane also flew him to Berlin in 1987, where — in the shadow of the Berlin Wall — he made the famous appeal to Gorbachev to "tear down this wall."

Just before the retirement of SAM 27000, President George W. Bush used the plane for the first and only time, making a round-trip flight from Waco to San Antonio, Texas, on August 29, 2001. Speaking to an American Legion annual convention, Bush noted that SAM 27000 "will carry no more presidents, but it will carry forever the spirit of American democracy." The president also noted the plane's special relationship to the Reagan years: "It will remind us of Ronald Reagan's achievements for peace and international security."[3]

On this occasion, President Bush was joined by former Air Force One crewmen: Ralph Albertazzie, President Nixon's pilot; Bob Ruddick, President Reagan's pilot; Danny Barr, President George H. W. Bush's pilot; and Chief Master Sergeant Joe Chappell, who had been the flight engineer on the plane's first flight, among others. In presidential missions covering more than one million miles, SAM 27000 had performed flawlessly, a testament to the high standards of the 89th Airlift Wing at Andrews Air Force Base. The historic plane made its final flight to California a few days later.

"I don't know what else I could have done." Mikhail Gorbachev
"You could have said yes." Ronald Reagan

proved to be a tough negotiator, but he shared with Gorbachev a desire to reach pivotal agreements on arms reduction.

West Berlin gave Reagan a unique platform to engage the larger issues of the Cold War, as it had offered his predecessor John F. Kennedy decades before; the city of Berlin remained arguably one of the most dangerous flash points in the confrontational East–West rivalry. In 1945, in the immediate aftermath of World War II, the victorious Allies had divided the former German capital into four occupation zones, and West Berlin — composed of the old British, French, and American sectors — existed as a democratic enclave situated deep inside communist East Germany. Abruptly, in 1961, the authorities in the eastern sector of Berlin constructed a twenty-eight-mile wall that divided the city in half.

The resulting Berlin Wall became a visible symbol of East–West tensions in the Cold War era. Flying on Air Force One, President Reagan arrived in the isolated city on

Below: President Ronald Reagan (*on left*) and Soviet leader Mikhail Gorbachev meet in Iceland in 1987, when Reagan asked Gorbachev to support his bold disarmament proposal.
Opposite: Like his predecessor John F. Kennedy, President Reagan came to Berlin to speak out against Soviet communism. Here, Reagan makes a speech near the Berlin Wall in front of the historic Brandenburg Gate on June 12, 1987, appealing to Gorbachev to "tear down this wall!"

June 12, 1987. At the Brandenburg Gate, just yards from the Wall, Reagan spoke boldly and resolutely: "General Secretary Gorbachev, if you seek peace, if you seek prosperity for the Soviet Union and Eastern Europe, if you seek liberalization: Come here to this gate! Mr. Gorbachev, open this gate! Mr. Gorbachev, tear down this wall!"[4]

Having challenged Gorbachev in a dramatic way, President Reagan remained open to a negotiated agreement with the Soviets on a large array of issues related to the arms race. Accordingly, he flew on Air Force One to Reykjavik, Iceland, in October 1987 to meet face-to-face with the Soviet leader. Gorbachev made an intriguing offer, proposing to eliminate all the Soviet Union's medium-range missiles deployed in Europe and, to the further surprise of the Reagan negotiating team, to cut the Soviet arsenal by nearly half. Implicit in the Gorbachev overture was the eventual total elimination of strategic weapons. The attractive offer, however, came with a price: the United States was to abandon the SDI program.

Writing in his memoirs, Reagan told how he reacted to this sudden demand: "I couldn't believe it and blew my top." For Reagan, the SDI was nonnegotiable, "an insurance policy to guarantee that the Soviets kept their commitments."[5] The angry president then announced, "The meeting is over, we're leaving." The following morning, as the two leaders made their exit, Gorbachev approached Reagan, saying, "I don't know what else I could have done." Reagan replied curtly, "You could have said yes."[6]

The Reykjavik summit ended abruptly because of the president's firm refusal to relinquish the SDI option, a posture that some on the American team found foolhardy given that SDI still was more a theory than a proven missile defense system. However, Reagan's determination, in the end, did not preclude a major breakthrough in the whole process of superpower negotiations: Gorbachev signed the milestone intermediate-range nuclear forces treaty in

"Look at me, I'm riding on Air Force One!" Nancy Reagan

December 1987. The INF treaty was unprecedented. For the first time, the two powers had agreed to eliminate an entire class of nuclear weapons.

On May 29, 1988, Air Force One landed at Moscow for a fourth encounter between Reagan and Gorbachev. First Lady Nancy Reagan joined her husband for this memorable journey. This was the president's first trip to the Soviet Union — to a center of world communism that he had earlier described as the "Evil Empire." The Moscow meeting allowed the two leaders to continue their dialogue on arms reduction and human rights. It also offered the president an opportunity to visit Red Square as a tourist, if briefly. When asked by a reporter if he still thought the Soviet Union was an evil empire, Reagan replied, "No, I was talking about another time, another era."[7] The reality of this altered world became highly visible after Reagan had left office, on November 9, 1989, when the Berlin Wall was breached and thousands poured into West Berlin from the communist sector — a symbolic moment in the rapid collapse of communism in Eastern Europe.

On board Air Force One, Reagan enjoyed the privacy of his forward cabin, where he spent considerable time; he also made regular visits to the senior staff lounge for meetings with his aides. The president seldom slept on flights, even long-distance journeys. Life on the Reagan Air Force One was not without its lighter side, as in the case of his 1985 trip to West Germany. En route to the airport, a group of teenagers "mooned" the motorcade, prompting Reagan to remark upon departure — with his hands spread apart — that those kids had "smiles this big."[8]

First Lady Nancy Reagan shared her husband's enthusiasm for Air Force One. When SAM 27000 was dispatched to California to transport the Reagan family to Washington for the inauguration, she had her first opportunity to fly on the presidential plane. "During our flight to Washington,"

Opposite: President Reagan, accompanied by the First Lady Nancy Reagan, enjoys a glass of champagne with members of the press corps and White House press spokesman Larry Speakes (*third from left*) on a trip to West Germany, June 11, 1982.
Above: On a trip to China in May 1984, President Reagan visits the cockpit of Air Force One. Reagan often chatted with the cockpit crew on long-distance flights.

she later reported, "Ronnie read reports and attended to paper work, while I kept busy writing letters to friends back home, on Air Force One letterhead. Look at me, I'm riding on Air Force One!"[9] The Reagans shared with other presidential couples the awe and excitement of being frequent flyers on the world's most fabled airplane.

John Hughes, an aide to Secretary of State George Shultz, observed that traveling with President Reagan was not always glamorous. For certain, there were the perks associated with Air Force One — souvenirs with the presidential seal, Air Force stewards delivering drinks, and the prestige and luxury associated with the plane's lifestyle — but Hughes noted that "the president would be up front in his cabin and you would be in the back with the rest of the entourage reading cables and clearing speeches and press statements and trying to catch a little sleep."[10]

Reagan routinely greeted guests and staff on each flight, a practice that earned him a reputation for unfailing courtesy on presidential flights. Hughes echoed this

Marine One: The Presidential Helicopters

Eisenhower Inaugurates the Era of Vertical Flight in White House Air Operations

Vertical flight became part of the saga of presidential travel in July 1957, when Dwight Eisenhower went aloft in a Bell H-13J Ranger helicopter as part of a Civil Defense exercise called "Operation Alert." Air Force major Joseph E. Barrett, a veteran airman with combat experience in both World War II and Korea, was at the controls on this maiden helicopter flight by an American president. For the ride, Eisenhower positioned himself on the rear seat, accompanied only by one Secret Service agent. For safety, a second helicopter flew escort, with Eisenhower's personal physician and a second Secret Service agent on board.

As an enthusiastic golfer, President Eisenhower prompted some to speculate that the helicopter would soon be the prime vehicle to transport the president to and from golf courses. These tongue-in-cheek anxieties proved unwarranted; in time, the helicopter earned a place in presidential travel as an efficient mode of transport for short shuttle flights or to reach remote areas. Eisenhower, in fact, proved to be only an occasional passenger on helicopters. In September 1957 he flew out of Newport, Rhode Island, on a Marine Sikorsky UH-34D Seahorse helicopter. Typically, Eisenhower flew on the larger UH-34D types, while the smaller Ranger types were reserved for VIPs. In time, the marines assumed the exclusive task of providing helicopter service for the White House.

The U.S. Marine Corps had activated its first helicopter squadron in December 1947. The squadron's mission in the late 1940s was to test a variety of helicopters, in anticipation of adapting vertical flight to marine air operations. Working out of the Marine Corps Air Station at Quantico,

Top: President Eisenhower waits to board a helicopter, which was then operated by the U.S. Air Force. *Center:* President Eisenhower and French President Charles de Gaulle (*left*) disembark Marine One at Eisenhower's Gettysburg farm on April 24, 1960. *Opposite:* President Eisenhower (*right*) and guests prepare to depart on board Marine One.

Virginia, this unit became known as Helicopter Squadron HMX-1: (H) helicopter; (M) marine; (X) experimental. The HMX pilots initially flew nine Piasecki HRP-1 and six Sikorsky HO3S-1 helicopters."

In the Eisenhower years, as helicopter technology advanced in the 1950s, military planners saw the manifest potential of vertical flight for White

House operations. The president's 1957 helicopter flight demonstrated his confidence in the essential safety of the new flight technology. Helicopters became a convenient and swift conveyance for Eisenhower to reach the presidential retreat at Camp David or his own farm in Gettysburg, Pennsylvania.

In the Cold War years of the 1950s, security advisers to Eisenhower gave thoughtful attention to the helicopter as a possible evacuation vehicle in a national emergency. The federal government, as a precautionary measure, had constructed special underground bunkers located outside Washington, D.C., to shield the president and his cabinet in case of a nuclear attack. During one evacuation exercise, Eisenhower rode in his limousine to the command center, for safety reasons, while his cabinet flew in a helicopter. The fact that the cabinet members arrived ahead of the president prompted a quest to find a reliable helicopter for use by the president.

In time, helicopters flying out of Quantico became known as "Marine One" when carrying the president. While the marines ultimately gained the exclusive franchise for presidential vertical flight, the air force and the army's Executive Flight Detachment had been part of the White House vertical flight operations. The latter, in fact, had been given the mandate to provide emergency evacuation for the president, his family, and other key officials. The army unit existed from 1958 to 1973.

In the late 1950s, both marine and army helicopter units flew Sikorsky CH-34 Choctaws (the military version of the Sikorsky S-58). These military helicopters had a crew of two and could carry twelve passengers. Slow by modern standards, the durable and reliable Chocktaws cruised at 95 miles

"Oh, if you are to be in the same helicopter, of course I will go!" Nikita Khrushchev

per hour and boasted a range of some 270 miles.

In 1963, the marines purchased Sikorsky CH-3 helicopters, which quickly set a standard for marine air operations. This particular helicopter was originally designed for the navy as the SH-3 Sea King. The HH-3E — as the "Jolly Green Giant" — later won fame in Vietnam as a troop carrier and liaison aircraft. This helicopter represented a new milestone in performance: a cruising speed of 150 miles per hour and a range of 465 miles.

For a time in the 1970s, President Nixon made use of a Bell UH-1-D, which could carry up to eleven passengers in its larger variant. The UH-1 Huey possessed two engines, which afforded a considerable margin of safety in the event of an engine breakdown.

Today, the U.S. Marine Corps Helicopter Squadron One (HMX-1) is a vital and essential part of transporting the president, the vice president, and foreign leaders. Marine helicopters routinely operate from the White House grounds, but these same helicopters have been flown in such widely separated places as Britain's Windsor Castle, Japan's Akasaka Palace, and the Demilitarized Zone in South Korea.

The executive flight operations of HMX-1, what the air unit calls the "white side" of its mission, flies two modern helicopter types: the Sikorsky VH-3D Sea King and the VH-60N Whitehawk. In the parlance of presidential travel, these helicopters are known as the "White Tops." Both the VH-3D and the VH-60N were designed so the rotors could be folded for loading on a C-5A Galaxy transport, to allow marine helicopters to serve the president on long domestic and foreign trips.

The VH-3D has a single main rotor and two turbine engines. The crew consists of a pilot, co-pilot, and crew chief. The interior cabin is temperature controlled and shares many of the interior appointments of an executive aircraft. This helicopter has been a mainstay in HMX-1 operations for over a quarter century. This particular helicopter has earned a reputation for reliability, with a cruising speed of 131 miles per hour and a range of 450 nautical miles. The presidential helicopter is a familiar presence on the White House grounds with its distinctive green and white livery, glistening exterior, and presidential seal.[12]

The Marine One VH-60N, as an executive transport, may carry as many as ten passengers. The helicopter typically flies with a crew consisting of a pilot, co-pilot, communications system operator, and crew chief. Marine One never flies solo; a second or spare helicopter flies as a decoy to confuse any would-be terrorist. Marine One is an essential component of the presidential travel scene. President George W. Bush aptly observed that the marine helicopters in White House service were not a perk: "I really view it as a part of the presidency because it enables me to get from point A to point B without inconveniencing a lot of my fellow Americans."[13]

Opposite: President Johnson saddles up to Marine One on his ranch in Texas in July 1966. *Clockwise from upper middle:* Marine One makes a stop at the Capitol on July 1, 1973; President Clinton and North Carolina governor Jim Hunt survey flood damage on September 20, 1999; President George W. Bush returns to the White House on March 27, 2003, after a two-day summit at Camp David with British prime minister Tony Blair; President Reagan and First Lady Nancy Reagan receive a warm welcome on the White House lawn from their dog, Millie, on April 20, 1987; President George H. W. Bush waves to the press before boarding Marine One on October 12, 1989; President Jimmy Carter, Anwar el-Sadat (*center*), and First Lady Rosalynn Carter return to the White House from Camp David on February 5, 1978; President Carter makes a trip to Three Mile Island, Pennsylvania, on board Marine One on April 1, 1979; and Richard Nixon disembarks Marine One onto the USS *Saratoga* off the coast of Naples, Italy, on September 29, 1970.

relaxed ambience on Air Force One when he described his own encounters with the president: "When you engaged in one-on-one conversation with him, he was focused on you completely. He was interested in whomever he met. . . . He was friendly, not afflicted by the pomp and ego of lesser inhabitants of the White House. He was perpetually courteous."[14]

Sometimes, Hughes recalled, he found himself on a second presidential plane assigned to accompany Reagan and his official party on Air Force One. There were pleasant surprises, such as occupying the unused presidential cabin, but this prestigious space could also have its downside. One trip to Latin America included a short and unscheduled stopover in Honduras. While the president, aboard Air Force One, landed for an impromptu meeting at the airport, those on the second presidential aircraft circled above. In time, Hughes remembered, "those of us on [the

Above, left: **Four U.S. presidents — left to right, Nixon, Reagan, Ford, and Carter — raise a toast at the White House on October 8, 1981. Later, Nixon, Ford, and Carter flew on Reagan's Air Force One to Egypt to attend the funeral of Anwar el-Sadat.**
Right: **President Ronald Reagan and Nancy Reagan board Marine One on January 20, 1989, at the Capitol for the inauguration of George H. W. Bush.**

backup aircraft] grew hungry for the steaks we knew were on the menu." The air force stewards, however, were reluctant to serve the meals. When asked why, a steward whispered, "We're not allowed to serve you until Air Force One has taken off. Should anything go wrong, and the president had to transfer to this backup plane, you'd have eaten the president's dinner."[15]

The assassination of Egyptian president Anwar Sadat in October 1981 set the stage for a unique flight on Air Force One. On the advice of his security advisers and in response to widespread fears for his safety, Reagan decided not to attend Sadat's funeral in Egypt. As an alternative, he made Air Force One available for a special delegation that included high-ranking congressional figures and former presidents Nixon, Ford, and Carter. Secretary of State Alexander Haig led the official party from Washington. Taking full advantage of the perks associated with his

"You can invite anyone you want to lunch or dinner, and chances are they'll come." Ronald Reagan

leadership of the delegation, Haig co-opted the presidential cabin on Air Force One for the long flight to Egypt, leaving Reagan's predecessors to seek out more modest seats on the presidential aircraft. It was a rare moment indeed to find three former occupants of the White House traveling together in what might be called VIP steerage.

Toward the end of the Reagan years, the U.S. Air Force launched a drive to replace the two VC-137Cs in presidential service. SAM 27000, Reagan's trusted Boeing 707 design — like its predecessor, SAM 26000 — had become increasingly obsolescent with the passing of time. There were concerns over the age of the airframe, along with the pressing need to upgrade the presidential communications suite, among other technical modernization priorities. Initially there was some interest in the McDonnell Douglas DC-10 and the Lockheed L1011 Tristar, but the final nod went to the Boeing Company for two 747-200B jumbo jets. Both aircraft, designated VC-25A, were scheduled for delivery to Andrews in 1988 and 1989, respectively. But problems arose in the production of the specially designed presidential aircraft, forcing delays and leading to substantial cost overruns. As it turned out, President Reagan's second term ended before he had an opportunity to fly on the new Air Force One.

For the Reagans, the final flight on Air Force One came after the inauguration of George H. W. Bush in January 1989. The Reagans flew home to California on the familiar presidential plane, a highly emotional experience for the couple. In her memoirs, Nancy Reagan remembered those last moments aloft: "On Air Force One, the pilot, who was flying his last trip too, came back to give us a beautiful picture of the White House and a lovely inscription from the crew."[16] The Reagan era on SAM 27000 concluded with a visit of the now former president with press in the rear compartment of the plane, an occasion where the crew served cake and champagne.

President George H. W. Bush and First Lady Barbara Bush depart on Air Force One from Maxwell Air Force Base in Montgomery, Alabama, in January 1990.

George H. W. Bush

As Ronald Reagan's vice president and heir, George Herbert Walker Bush presided over the turbulent last years of the Cold War, witnessed the final collapse of the Soviet Union, and led a coalition of nations to expel Saddam Hussein's Iraqi army from Kuwait in the first Gulf War. His presidential tenure coincided with some momentous events in history.

President Bush discovered happily that his term in office also saw the arrival of a new generation of presidential aircraft, the delivery of two Boeing 747-200B jumbo jets. In practical terms, the presidential 747s offered Bush an awe-inspiring mode of transport for the conduct of foreign affairs at a critical moment in history.

As president, Bush stood in sharp contrast to his predecessor both in personality and in his approach to politics. The son of a United States senator, Bush came from a patrician New England family, although as an adult he established strong ties to his adopted state of Texas. He had served as a navy pilot in the Pacific during World War II. His post-war life led to a remarkable political career

as a Texas congressman, the director of the Central Intelligence Agency, and ambassador to the United Nations. Unlike Reagan, Bush was not known as a "conviction" politician whose style of leadership was strongly identified with conservative ideological principles. In the public arena he appeared highly pragmatic, always preferring compromise to confrontation, and in the crucible of international affairs he displayed considerable skills in the art of diplomacy.

Taking office in 1989, Bush found himself walking a tightrope, encouraging the disintegration of communism in Poland, Czechoslovakia, and East Germany, while at the same time seeking to reassure Gorbachev of his intent to refrain from exploiting unfairly the growing crisis in the communist world. The unscripted events associated with the demise of the Cold War posed unique problems for the president.

Like Reagan, Bush managed to develop a close working relationship with Gorbachev, participating in his first summit with the Soviet leader in December 1989 aboard U.S. and Soviet naval vessels in the storm-tossed waters off Malta. This meeting furthered the cause of détente between the two superpowers. But events would soon overtake the familiar process of Cold War summitry: the Soviet Union, in fact, was headed for disintegration. Despite the

ideological pretensions of the communist regime and all the efforts of Gorbachev at liberalization, the red flag of the Soviet Union was lowered from the Kremlin in late 1991.

Bush often flew on Air Force One during his single term in office, using the presidential plane for high-profile journeys to attend summit meetings with Gorbachev in Helsinki and Moscow. He also employed the presidential plane for a special trip to Saudi Arabia to visit American troops on the eve of the Gulf War. As president, Bush reaffirmed the essential role of Air Force One in the conduct of foreign affairs, a tradition that began in the Eisenhower years.

President Bush took his first domestic flight, to Kansas, on the new Air Force One — a Boeing 747-200B — on September 6, 1990. The following day he made a second journey, this time to Helsinki, Finland, for a summit meeting with Gorbachev. These flights demonstrated the quantum leap in technological sophistication and comfort now incorporated into presidential air travel. As the new incarnation of Air Force One, the presidential 747s proved to be problem free and inspired awe in those who encountered them.

The contract for the new presidential 747s had been given to Boeing in July 1986, with the hope that the new

Air Force One would be ready in time to fly Ronald Reagan home after the completion of his second term in January 1989. However, the new presidential aircraft entered service in the early months of the Bush administration after many delays. While under construction in Everett, Washington (with the interior appointments installed at the Boeing plant in Wichita, Kansas), the planes attracted great curiosity, given their special features and intended use. The press also reported that the planes were delivered to Andrews at extraordinary cost, well beyond the original estimates.

President Bush viewed his new presidential plane with no small amount of pride and satisfaction. The new 747s dwarfed the earlier generation of 707s flown by his predecessors in the White House. The president enjoyed the spacious private quarters of the forward cabin, and he and First Lady Barbara Bush took some delight in the fact that the press area was segregated in the rear of the fuselage: "Every once in a while," Bush observed, "a venturesome press person would leave the comfortable pen in the back and wander forth, hoping to glean a tidbit of color or substance. We used to politely send them back from whence they came. It was better that way, for leaks seemed to spring more at that altitude."[17]

The new Air Force One also evoked awe in the press.

Top, left: President Bush tries out a comfortable chair on the new presidential 747 on September 6, 1990.
Right: The president relaxes with the crew of the new Air Force One on November 3, 1990.
Above: President Bush waves as he departs on his inaugural flight on the new Air Force One on September 6, 1990.

"To get to the plane you have to walk up to it, which is the only way truly to appreciate its immensity," Joel Achenbach of the *Washington Post* wrote. "It is hard to believe it can get into the air. The engines are the size of locomotives. I walked up to the rear stairwell and took a seat in the small press cabin at the back of the plane. The interior design isn't like a normal plane — it's divided into rooms rather than cabins, with many of the spaces having no windows on one side, probably for security reasons. The President can go anywhere on the plane and still be away from a window."[18]

Bush, who routinely conferred with his staff while in flight, found the huge conference room on the presidential 747 an ideal place for meetings. There were also occasions when he directed his press secretary, Marlin Fitzwater, to summon the press from their cordoned-off quarters in the rear fuselage to the conference room for an impromptu discussion. Bush discovered that the conference room always served as the locale for birthday parties: "The able crew of AF1 must have had a birthday-detection sensor hidden somewhere, for no top staffer, no gofer, no middle-range policy wonk who had a birthday could escape the inevitable 'Surprise, Surprise!' gathering in the conference room . . . . Then the cake would be cut, and sparkling wine (of recent vintage) would be poured. Most of the birthday

George H. W. Bush, then vice president, naps on board Air Force One with his wife, Barbara, during the presidential campaign of 1984.

"What's wrong with being a boring kind of guy?"
President George H. W. Bush

Special Features of the New Air Force One
The Acquisition of Twin Boeing 747s Radically Transforms Presidential Air Travel

The modern incarnation of Air Force One became a reality in September 1990, when President George H. W. Bush took the maiden presidential flight on the first Boeing 747-200 jumbo jet delivered to the 89th Airlift Wing at Andrews Air Force Base. Andrew Rosenthal of the *New York Times* covered the event, reporting that the new high-tech presidential plane was "crammed with electronics — from devices mounted over the engines to fool heat-seeking missiles, to the communications center that can instantly reach any part of the world."[19] Rosenthal also alerted his readers that each high-tech plane cost about $181.5 million, with the total cost of two 747s and a huge hangar at Andrews Air Force Base topping out at $410 million. Later that same month, Bush flew the new plane to a Helsinki summit with Mikhail Gorbachev, offering the international community its first look at the new airborne White House.

Two Boeing 747-200B jets, in fact, entered service in the 1990s, being designated by the U.S. Air Force as VC-25As, with tail numbers 28000 and 29000. Either plane assumes the call sign "Air Force One" when flying the president of United States. Both aircraft came to Andrews bearing the distinctive blue, silver, and white colors first adopted for John F. Kennedy's fabled Air Force One (SAM 26000) in 1962, a striking livery created by famed industrial designer Raymond Loewy.

The performance profile for the modern presidential 747s is indeed impressive. Tall as a six-story building and with a fuselage as a long as a football field, Air Force One weighs about 833,000 pounds. This behemoth plane, however, is an agile and speedy flying machine, powered by four General Electric CF-6-80C2B1 jet engines, each rated with 56,700 pounds of thrust. On Air Force One, a modern president cruises to his destination at a speed in excess of six hundred miles per hour.

Unlike commercial 747s, Air Force One can be refueled while in flight. Such a capability offers the president, in a national emergency, virtually unlimited range.

The specially designed interior of the modern Air Force One offers the president privacy and his official party a real measure of comfort and luxury. This stress on special features is not new: The tradition goes back to the first official plane assigned to a U.S. president in 1945, the C-54 *Sacred Cow.* For wheelchair-bound Franklin Delano Roosevelt, the use of a special elevator to board that plane dictated a design priority. This precedent cast a long shadow over the interior design of presidential planes, if now less personalized.

The presidential 747s are similar in most respects, each offering some four thousand square feet of floor space for the interior compartments. The appointments are first class, but in the words

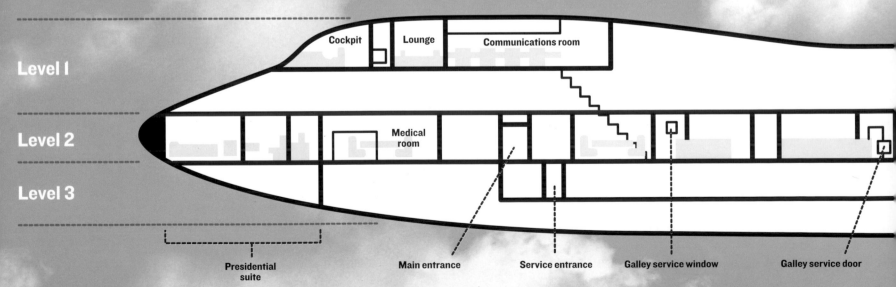

Level 1 — Cockpit — Lounge — Communications room

Level 2 — Medical room

Level 3

Presidential suite — Main entrance — Service entrance — Galley service window — Galley service door

Level 1

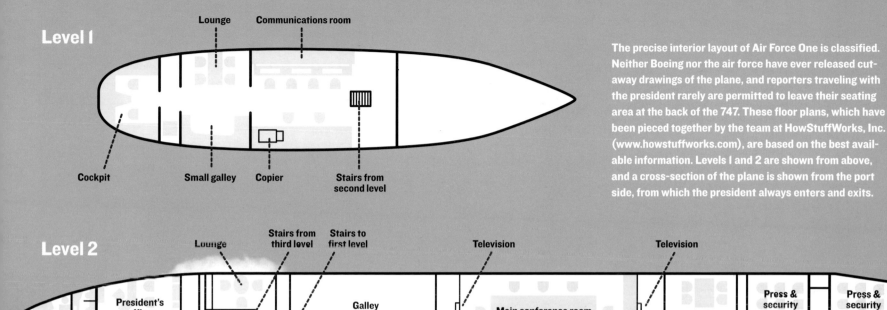

Lounge

Communications room

Cockpit

Small galley

Copier

Stairs from second level

The precise interior layout of *Air Force One* is classified. Neither Boeing nor the air force have ever released cutaway drawings of the plane, and reporters traveling with the president rarely are permitted to leave their seating area at the back of the 747. These floor plans, which have been pieced together by the team at HowStuffWorks, Inc. (www.howstuffworks.com), are based on the best available information. Levels 1 and 2 are shown from above, and a cross-section of the plane is shown from the port side, from which the president always enters and exits.

Level 2

Lounge

Stairs from third level

Stairs to first level

Television

Television

President's office

Galley

Main conference room

Work room

Press & security seating

Press & security seating

Medical room

Presidential suite

Main entrance

Stairs from third level

Restroom

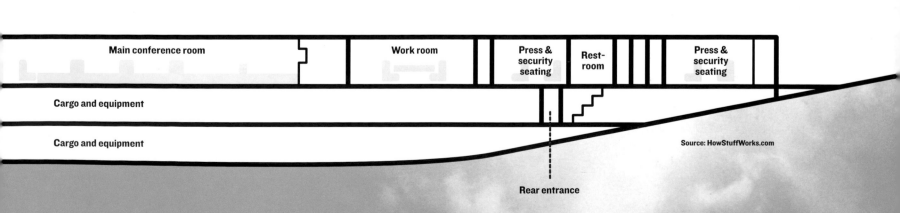

Main conference room

Work room

Press & security seating

Rest-room

Press & security seating

Cargo and equipment

Cargo and equipment

Rear entrance

Source: HowStuffWorks.com

Boeing 747-200B

Crew: 26
Capacity: 102
Length: 231 feet, 10 inches
Height: 63 feet, 5 inches
Wingspan: 195 feet, 8 inches
Speed: 630 miles per hour (Mach 0.92)
Ceiling: 45,100 feet
Maximum takeoff weight: 833,000 pounds
Fuel capacity: 53,611 gallons
Range: 7,800 statute miles
Thrust: 56,700 pounds, each engine

"It is hard to believe i

can get into the air. The engines are the size of locomotives."

Joel Achenbach, *Washington Post*

"The thing I miss about Air Force One is they don't lose my luggage." George H. W. Bush

of President George H. W. Bush, the plane is "presidential — that is, not opulent or grand, but big and efficient."[20] The interior could be described as something reminiscent of a corporate executive jet or even a modern and well-appointed hotel. Air Force One can accommodate up to seventy passengers.

Other features of Air Force One suggest quality service and a penchant for self-sufficiency. Two full galleys stocked with a large quantity of fresh and frozen food allow the crew to serve as many as one hundred passengers at one sitting. Steps were also taken to fashion a modern medical facility, equipped with a fold-out operating table. The staff routinely includes a doctor on board to assure the president proper care in the face of any emergency.

The modern Air Force One possesses built-in retractable stairways, a design feature eliminating the need to use mobile airport stairs or to fly in special stairs to fit the plane. The stairways, which allow easy access to the outside tarmac upon landing, are linked to connecting stairways and other compartments on the multilevel plane. The president's own compartment is situated in the forward nose section and opens to this internal network of stairs and passageways.

The most fascinating dimension of Air Force One, of course, is its high-tech systems, aspects of which remain highly classified. The secrecy of the most critical avionics and defensive systems is critical to the safety of the president. The plane is fitted with electronic countermeasures, a defensive shield against hostile attack. Even the elaborate wiring of the presidential 747s has been shielded against the effects of electromagnetic

pulse — the wave of energy released in a nuclear explosion. As threats of presidential assassination have given way to additional threats from terrorists, the U.S. Air Force has recognized the threat of anti-aircraft infrared guided missiles. Accordingly, advanced defensive capabilities are now a part of Air Force One. For example, it has been reported that FAA-certificated ALQ-204 Matador Infrared Countermeasures (IRCM) jammers are now standard equipment on presidential 747s, as one component in an array of high-tech defenses.[21]

While the current Boeing 747s in presidential service are highly regarded for their utility and impressive symbolism, they came to Andrews only after delays (they were intended to be operational before Ronald Reagan left office in 1989) and unanticipated cost, the actual price tag having wildly exceeded original estimates. In terms of operational costs, one GAO estimate in 1999 put the cost of flying Air Force One at $34,400 per hour, not to mention the cost of transport planes for presidential limos and equipment and crew training. When one adds Marine One to the tally, perhaps another $5,000 to $6,000 an hour, the actual cost of presidential air travel remains as high as it is difficult to determine with any accuracy. The bipartisan rationale for such air travel is often spirited, suggesting that Air Force One is now a practical and indispensable arm of the American presidency.[22]

Interior views of Air Force One during the presidency of George H. W. Bush, showing the president's office and the conference room. These photographs were taken on October 10, 1990, shortly after President Bush took possession of the new 747 aircraft. The bottom photo at near right shows the president talking to members of the crew on November 3, 1990.

President George H. W. Bush dines with American troops in Saudi Arabia during Desert Shield, November 23, 1990.

people seemed pleased to have me speak and leave. They could relax better that way."[23]

The conference room, as Bush remembered it, became the locale for many other activities on long flights, from gin rummy games to informal conversations and socializing. He also recalled this precinct of Air Force One as a great place for the staff to sleep, with the wall-to-wall couches serving as improvised beds. For those seeking entertainment, there were the movies: "You simply turn on your TV," Bush observed with no small amount of amazement, "then call upstairs on your private phone, then watch a sputter or two and on comes Goldie Hawn or Sally Field, or Arnold or Bruce or Demi. Never Madonna, but who cares. Everyone on the plane has access to AF1's library of movies."[24]

President Bush and his staff also had easy phone access on his new plane. "When it comes to phone calls from AF1," he observed, "there is monumental glamour involved. Everyone knows such a call is a prestige builder. Romances can be cemented forever by just one call from AF1."[25] Like Jimmy Carter, he was not averse to using the presidential plane to impress congressmen and senators, allowing them the freedom to call their constituents from

Air Force One with maximum impact. In the decade of the 1990s and beyond, the new presidential planes became effective backdrops for political campaigning, a practice that proved irresistible for all occupants of the White House, regardless of party affiliation.

In July 1991, President Bush flew to the Soviet Union on Air Force One for a meeting with Mikhail Gorbachev, arriving at Moscow's Sheremetyevo airport to be greeted by a small honor guard. In the days that followed, the two leaders met in the ornate St. Catherine's Hall in the Kremlin for the signing of the Strategic Arms Reduction Treaty. Notwithstanding the pomp and significance of the occasion, the Soviet regime was in turmoil that summer amidst rumors of a plot to overthrow Gorbachev. The rumors became a reality in October when a coup attempt was foiled — a political crisis that brought Boris Yeltsin to prominence and set the stage for the collapse of the regime at the end of that year. Much of Bush's time and energy was devoted to handling the extraordinary events of 1991.

While visiting Moscow, President Bush flew on Air Force One from Sheremetyevo airport to Kiev, the capital of Ukraine, which was then an integral part of the Soviet Union. Bush had agreed to take on a most unusual group of passengers: Soviet vice president Gennadi Yanayev; a protocol officer from the Kremlin; a KGB secret police colonel; Viktor Komplektov, the Soviet ambassador to the United States; and a small group of escorts selected by Gorbachev's government. While en route to Kiev on the two-hour flight, the Soviet guests were quartered in the commodious conference room, where they were treated to a special lunch. Yanayev took great pleasure in drinking scotch supplied by the plane's galley, but complained bitterly about the strict smoking ban on Air Force One.

Yanayev was inattentive to Bush's overtures to discuss policy or even to engage in small talk, so the president decided to give the surly Soviet official a tour of the plane,

Far left: President Bush exits Air Force One on April 30, 1992, at Columbus, Ohio.
Left: On his first domestic trip in the new Air Force One, President Bush visited Topeka, Kansas, on September 6, 1990.

showing him the high-tech communications center, the presidential suite and bathroom, and the automatic window shades. In the face of all this ultramodern gadgetry, Yanayev merely responded "Very nice" or "Very interesting."[26] In October 1991, Yanayev would play a central role in the abortive plot to remove Gorbachev from power, the event that set the stage for the collapse of the Soviet Union and the emergence of Yeltsin as the new Russian leader.

A signature moment in the presidency of George H. W. Bush was the Gulf War of 1991. Just two months before launching Operation Desert Storm, Bush flew on Air Force One to the Persian Gulf to spend the Thanksgiving holiday with soldiers and sailors deployed to expel Saddam Hussein's Iraqi army from Kuwait. He visited military personnel on shore in Saudi Arabia and on naval vessels stationed in the Persian Gulf. Air Force One had allowed President Bush to make direct contact with his armed forces on the eve of war, extending in a literal way the symbolic power of the presidency to a remote part of the globe.

Air Force One in the 1990s gave Bush and his successors immediate access to unfolding events in international affairs, a global reach unthinkable a generation earlier.

Chapter Six Flight Paths to a New Century

Bill Clinton and George W. Bush

AIR FORCE ONE OPERATIONS in the 1990s became more sophisticated as the scope and purpose of presidential travel enlarged to meet the demands of the modern presidency. President Bill Clinton's use of Air Force One, if not a departure from the precedents established by his predecessors, nevertheless prompted occasional controversy. During this decade the twin presidential 747s flew on many flight paths, serving purposes of the state and the domestic political agenda of the chief executive.

The presidential election of 1992 came after the abrupt end of the Cold War and after the popularity of George H. W. Bush in the wake of the first Gulf War had proven illusory. Consequently, foreign policy quickly gave way to an electoral cycle dominated by domestic issues, opening the way for Arkansas governor William Jefferson Clinton to win the presidential prize. His informal campaign slogan, "It's the economy, stupid," took full advantage of Bush's perceived inattention to this growing public concern. This issue resonated with the voters, and Bush suffered defeat at the polls as a consequence.

Clinton had grown up in poverty, but displayed great drive and intelligence in his remarkable rise to political power. Trained as a lawyer, he showed considerable skills in winning and sustaining political power. As president, Clinton was blessed with a vibrant economy and managed

Opposite: **President Bill Clinton and First Lady Hillary Clinton prepare to board Air Force One on June 15, 1995. The two presidential 747s were deployed on September 6, 1990 (SAM 28000), and March 26, 1991 (SAM 29000).**
Above: **Bill and Hillary Clinton wave as they enter Air Force One on June 29, 1996.**

to weather the dramatic Republican congressional victories in 1994, controversial government shutdowns over the budget, and a sequence of scandals that resulted in an impeachment trial at the end of his tenure. Clinton emerged as the first Democratic president to win reelection since Franklin Delano Roosevelt.

President Clinton devoted considerable energy to foreign policy, which meant frequent use of Air Force One to travel to far-flung locales, most memorably to China, to pursue his diplomatic goals. His foreign policy centered on an active program to promote peace throughout the world. Early on he faced a serious crisis in the Balkans, where the breakup of the old Yugoslav state set into motion a sequence of ethnic conflicts in Bosnia and Kosovo. In the case of Kosovo, the Clinton administration demonstrated a willingness to use air power and twenty thousand troops as peacemakers to achieve the president's diplomatic ends.

Clinton mobilized Air Force One in November 1995 to lead a delegation of high-ranking officials to fly to Israel for the funeral of assassinated Israeli prime minister Yitzhak Rabin. Two former presidents, Jimmy Carter and George H. W. Bush, accepted the invitation to accompany Clinton to Israel. George P. Shultz joined the delegation to represent his former boss, Ronald Reagan. Also on board Air Force One were Republican senator Bob Dole and House

What It Takes to Move the President

This graphic representation of a hypothetical presidential overseas trip shows how the president, his entourage and security, the accompanying press, and a wide variety of necessary equipment would be moved to a foreign location. With the focus of media coverage of such journeys on Air Force One itself, the massive logistics required are largely invisible to the public.

Five huge U.S. Air Force transports — two C-5s and three C-17s — carry equipment and personnel, including a large security contingent. The transports are refueled in flight by air force tankers, represented here by six KC-10s and KC-135s.

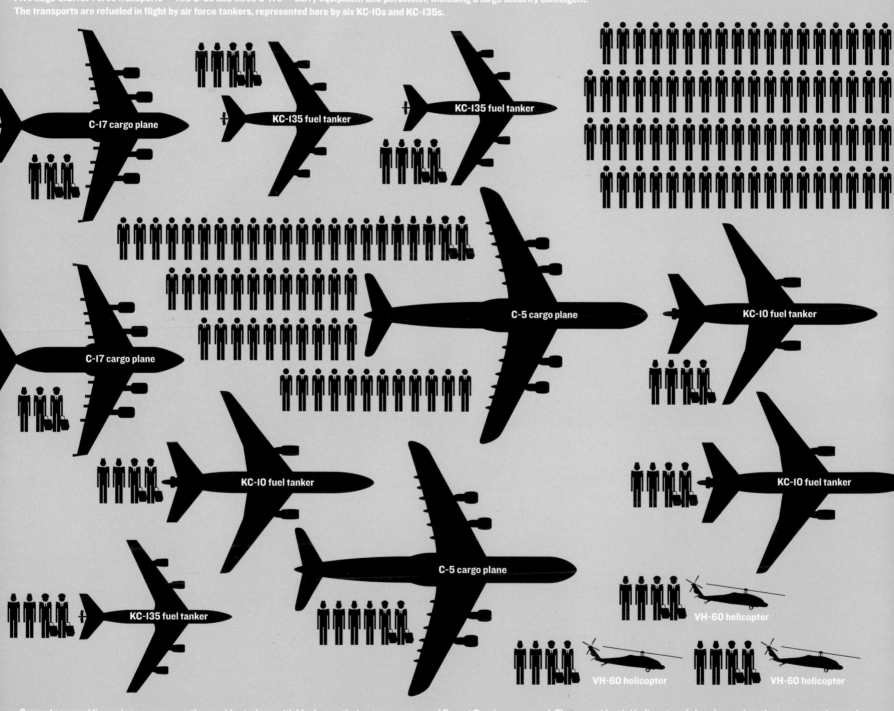

C-17 cargo plane

KC-135 fuel tanker

KC-135 fuel tanker

C-17 cargo plane

C-5 cargo plane

KC-10 fuel tanker

KC-10 fuel tanker

KC-10 fuel tanker

C-5 cargo plane

KC-135 fuel tanker

VH-60 helicopter

VH-60 helicopter

VH-60 helicopter

Several armored limousines accompany the president, along with black vans that carry weapons and Secret Service personnel. Three presidential helicopters (*above*) complete the transportation package.

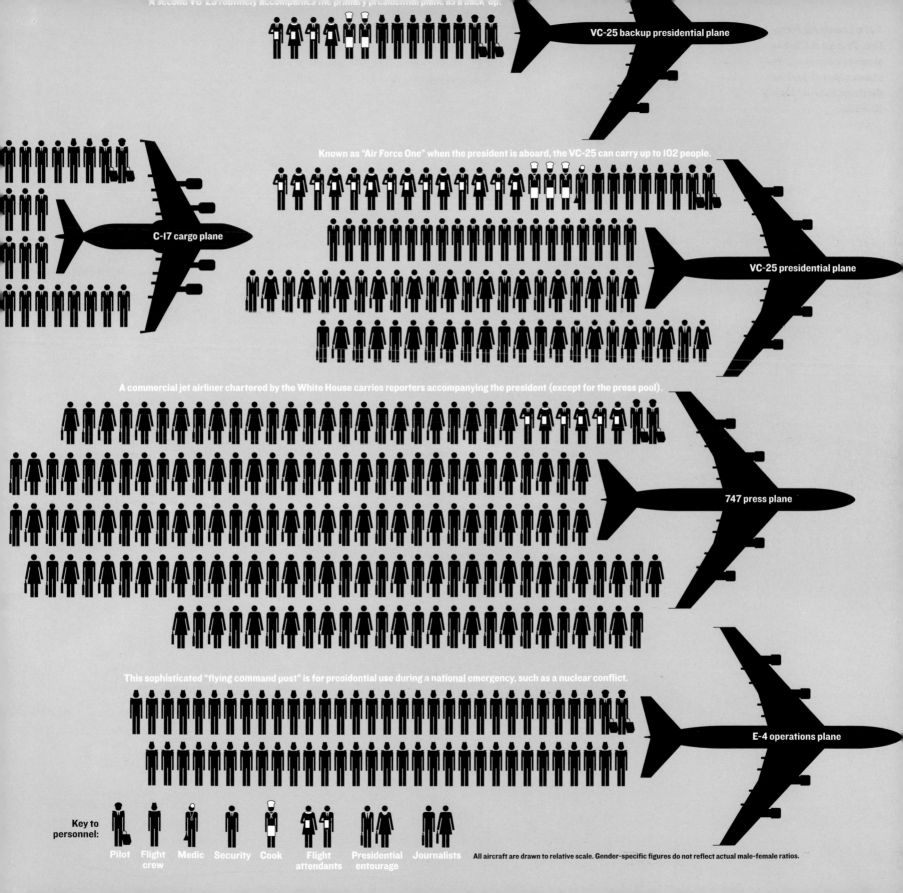

A second VC-25 routinely accompanies the primary presidential plane as a back-up.

VC-25 backup presidential plane

C-17 cargo plane

Known as "Air Force One" when the president is aboard, the VC-25 can carry up to 102 people.

VC-25 presidential plane

A commercial jet airliner chartered by the White House carries reporters accompanying the president (except for the press pool).

747 press plane

This sophisticated "flying command post" is for presidential use during a national emergency, such as a nuclear conflict.

E-4 operations plane

Key to personnel:

Pilot   Flight crew   Medic   Security   Cook   Flight attendants   Presidential entourage   Journalists

All aircraft are drawn to relative scale. Gender-specific figures do not reflect actual male-female ratios.

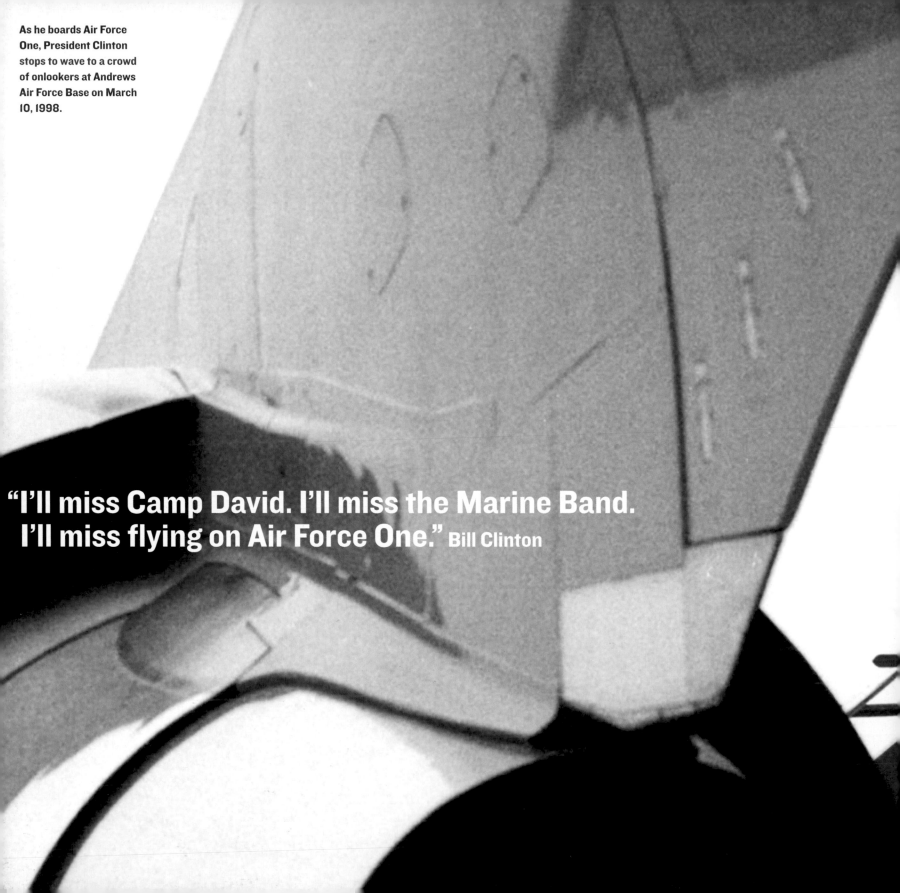

"I'll miss Camp David. I'll miss the Marine Band. I'll miss flying on Air Force One." Bill Clinton

On a highly controversial flight, President Clinton and a prestigious delegation travel on **Air Force One** together to attend the funeral of assassinated Israeli prime minister Yitzhak Rabin in November 1995. Pictured (*left to right*) are Congressman Tom Daschle; Senator Bob Dole; Speaker of the House Newt Gingrich; a crewman (standing); Gingrich's wife, Marianne; former Secretary of State George Shultz; and President Clinton (standing).

Speaker Newt Gingrich. It was rare to have such an ensemble of political luminaries on the presidential plane.

In the wake of this flight to Israel, a political row ensued over the charge that Newt Gingrich had been asked to exit Air Force One by a rear door. The truth about the obscure incident was lost in a swirl of charges and countercharges. Whatever actually happened on the journey to the Rabin funeral, Air Force One had unwittingly been co-opted as a stage for the ongoing partisan struggle between the president and his opponents in Congress.

Todd S. Purdum, writing for the *New York Times,* pointed to other "comic opera aspects" associated with the flight, which involved some twenty hours aloft. "The presidential cabin," Purdum noted, "is the only one with beds, leaving Mr. Bush, Mr. Carter, Mr. [Leon] Panetta [Clinton's chief of staff], and Secretary of State Warren M. Christopher to bunk together in reclining seats in the senior staff cabin. In the morning, lines formed for the

bathrooms. Mr. [Michael] McCurry [Clinton's press secretary] emerged to find Mr. Bush, toilet kit in hand. 'He had to take his turn,' Mr. McCurry said, 'like everyone else.'"[1]

President Clinton's highly publicized 1998 journey to China on Air Force One became an important milestone. No past presidential journey surpassed this one in terms of the fanfare, the cost, and the number of people folded into the presidential entourage. The China trip demonstrated anew how a chief executive could make lavish use of the presidential planes — with all their symbolism and prestige — to achieve political ends. Critics of the China trip complained that the Clinton administration had been guilty of excess. But defenders of the administration quickly countered that the extensive use of Air Force One and sister presidential planes had been a fixed aspect of White House leadership in modern times, regardless of the political party in power. Whatever the motives or the consequences, few argued with the notion that, on the eve of the twenty-first century, air travel had become an established feature of presidential leadership.

Clinton's trip to China mirrored the growing importance of Sino-American relations at the end of the twentieth century, and in most respects it represented a monumental logistics challenge when compared with Richard Nixon's pioneering trek to China in 1972. Air Force One flew into Chinese air space accompanied by two backup presidential aircraft. The enormous Clinton presidential entourage occupied all six hundred rooms at the posh Portman Ritz-Carlton in Shanghai upon arrival. A total of sixty vehicles made up the official motorcade as it moved through the Chinese capital, Beijing. This long trail of limousines and staff vehicles was deemed necessary to accommodate the official party consisting of six cabinet members, six members of Congress, scores of senior-level staff, and equal numbers of schedulers and press aides. Secretary of State Madeleine Albright typically traveled with a

The Fatal Crash of a Marine Helicopter
President Clinton's Flight on a Whitehawk Precedes a Deadly Crash

A marine corps helicopter crashed in a wooded area along the Potomac in Charles County, Maryland, on May 19, 1993. The following day, the *Washington Post* published a sketchy account of the incident, reporting that four marines died in the crash. Interest in the accident grew once it was learned that the downed helicopter was a VH-60N Whitehawk aircraft, belonging to the presidential helicopter fleet at Quantico marine base in Virginia.

The Marine VH-60N, fitted as an executive aircraft, served as a transport for the president, the vice president, and other high-ranking officials. The helicopter could accommodate ten passengers and a crew of four. The rotor blades of the VH-60N could be folded, if required, for transport on an Air Force C-5A/B. The helicopter belonged to Marine Helicopter Squadron One (HMX-1), an air unit responsible for presidential travel in coordination with the U.S. Air Force's 89th Airlift Wing at Andrews Air Force Base.

The marine helicopter took off from Quantico at 12:45 P.M. on May 19, crashing shortly afterwards in an area of forests and tobacco farms some thirty-five miles south of Washington, D.C. Reporters were barred from the scene, and armed marine guards quickly established a cordon around the crash site. There were also reports of a marine officer seizing a videotape with footage of the site, taken by a member of a local fire department. The tight security remained in effect until the wreckage was removed by helicopter. The U.S. Marine Corps reported that the helicopter had been on a maintenance flight when it crashed.

Later, one published account of the accident suggested that it was caused by a maintenance error, with improperly installed equipment leading to both engines on the aircraft flaming out.[2] Dee Dee Myers, President Clinton's press secretary, stated that the downed helicopter was a VH-60N and not one of the familiar VH-3 Sea King helicop-

President Clinton steps onto the deck of the USS *Theodore Roosevelt,* underway off the coast of Norfolk, Virginia, from a VH-60 Whitehawk helicopter on March 12, 1993. This is the helicopter that later crashed.

ters that normally operated from the grounds of the White House. She noted, "it is the [exact] helicopter that flew President [Clinton] to the [USS] *Roosevelt* when he visited the [aircraft] carrier." She went on to assure the public that "the Marine One the president flies is safe."[3]

The crash of the VH-60N represented one of the rare instances of mechanical failure related to any aircraft assigned to transport the president and high officials.

President Bill Clinton (*left*) meets with his staff in the conference room of Air Force One on a flight on December 4, 1994. U.N. ambassador Madeleine Albright sits to the right of Clinton.

"To a large extent it really is a job like other jobs." Bill Clinton

Hollywood and Air Force One: Fact vs. Fancy

Harrison Ford Fights Terrorists on a Fictional Air Force One

Hollywood has often brought images of American presidents to the silver screen. Presidents such as Abraham Lincoln, Woodrow Wilson, Franklin D. Roosevelt, and John F. Kennedy, among others, have often supplied the cinema with compelling story lines.

The 1997 blockbuster film *Air Force One* broke tradition by moving the stage from the White House to Air Force One, offering moviegoers a fictional modern president caught up in an airborne plot filled with action and international intrigue. Starring Harrison Ford (as the fictional president James Marshall) and Glenn Close (as his equally fictional vice president), the film features Kazakh terrorists seizing Air Force One, the symbol of American power. President Marshall manages to elude his would-be captors while on board the plane. In a sequence of heroic acts, Marshall thwarts the evil intentions of the hijackers. In a maelstrom of death and mayhem, the single-minded president, a former soldier, displays great agility, bravery, and James Bond–like survival skills to carry the day.

Fast-paced and suspense-filled, *Air Force One* blends implausible action scenes with authentic-looking sets. Director Wolfgang Peterson, a stickler for accurate detail, took great pains to evoke the ambience of the huge presidential plane. His past credits included *Das Boot*, the grim and realistic account of life on a German submarine in World War II. Peterson made full use of a huge Hollywood sound stage for his elaborate mock-ups of the plane's interior, the locale for the struggle between Marshall and the hijackers.

Peterson created a stunning adventure flick by

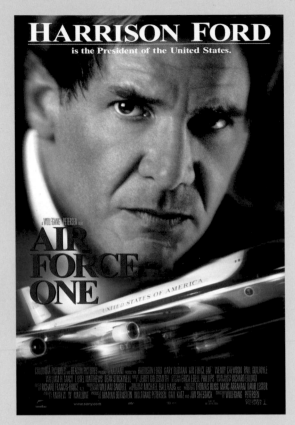

HARRISON FORD

is the President of the United States.

A WOLFGANG PETERSEN film

AIR FORCE ONE

UNITED STATES OF AMERICA

Harrison Ford as president was all this movie poster needed to advertise. The interior of Air Force One was convincingly recreated by art directors Nancy Patton, Carl Aldana, and Carl Stensel and set designers Peter Kelly, Karl Martin, Martha Johnson, Harry Otto, and Lynn Christopher. The film, which was released in July 1997, brought in nearly $173 million at the box office, placing it within the ranks of the eighty top-grossing movies.

combining models of Air Force One with actual flying scenes employing a full-scale Boeing 747, the latter hired from American International Airways. Other flying episodes required the use of U.S. Air Force fighters and transports. The AIA Boeing 747, as a flying prop, had to be painted with the authentic livery of Air Force One, but the sense of realism was convincing, as cinematic magic imitated life.

The paint job to transform the rented Boeing 747 into Air Force One cost more than $300,000, and to fly the plane Peterson hired Paul Bishop, an AIA pilot with more than 25,000 hours in his flight log.[4]

The use of an escape capsule on Harrison Ford's presidential plane gave a fanciful dimension to the story. Yet this most implausible of high-tech gadgetry appeared to become a possibility at the end of the 1990s, when rumors circulated that Russian president Vladimir Putin's new executive jet would be equipped with an escape module. Many wondered if real life may have imitated Hollywood.

While the plot for *Air Force One* appeared fanciful to even the most credulous moviegoer, the director's attentiveness to technical accuracy won wide praise when the film debuted. Informed aviation enthusiasts, however, noticed that the repainted AIA Boeing 747 lacked certain details of the original, in particular its telltale bulge on the nose (for aerial refueling) and the highly classified electronic gear fitted on its tail cone. The replica of the interior, set up on a huge sound stage, mirrored the presidential plane's layout of compartments, conference rooms, seats, windows, and communications equipment. This studied approach to reality also shaped the script, where steps were taken to incorporate into the dialogue the slang and nomenclature of air force operations.

In *Air Force One,* Hollywood sought to fashion a compelling tale of heroism, one involving a fictional president struggling with the real-life specter of terrorism. The use of images of Air Force One as the cinematic backdrop for the blockbuster movie suggests that the presidential plane has become a fixed part of the American imagination, a symbol of national power and prestige.

Above: President Marshall and his national security advisor Jack Doherty (played by Tom Everett, *left*), confer in a recreated Air Force One office. *Upper right, top:* President Marshall reassures his daughter, Alice (played by Liesel Matthews), that they are safe on board the plane. *Upper right, middle:* Film crew set up a shot of the fanciful escape pod. *Upper right, bottom:* The fictional president confronts a terrorist conspirator (played by Xander Berkeley) in a final scene of the movie. *Right:* Set designers for the movie transformed a commercial 747 into a replica of the presidential plane with its distinctive livery.

retinue of some thirty aides. The passenger manifest for China mushroomed with the addition of three hundred reporters, the required Secret Service agents, and other government officials mobilized as essential personnel for the odyssey.[5]

Clinton's press secretary, Mike McCurry, did not take an apologetic posture in explaining the alleged excesses, arguing that summitry — with all its trade and political ramifications — required a large number of government entities to participate in the multilevel discussions with Chinese authorities. "This is not just the president coming over to meet with President Jiang Zemin," McCurry insisted. "This is the government of the United States coming over to meet with the government of the People's Republic of China."[6]

Whatever the rationale for such a trip, modern presidential travel placed enormous burdens on White House planners and the various government agencies mandated to provide the president with adequate security measures. The exact numbers remain classified, but the trip to China involved hundreds of security and military personnel. The State Department supplied a cadre of Chinese-speaking

Top: **President Bill Clinton joins his wife, Hillary, and daughter, Chelsea, for an informal photograph at the Great Wall of China on June 28, 1998.**
Above: **While on his nine-day visit to China in 1998, President Clinton addressed university students in Beijing.**

translators. There were also at least five White House advance teams, each numbering as many as fifteen people. Each stop on the itinerary was surveyed and planned for in cooperation with the Chinese authorities. With Air Force One as the tip of the spear, President Clinton arrived in China not only with his entourage but, following established practice, with his own limousines and special mobile communications facilities.

Comparisons to previous trips to China by other presidents cast a light on the altered nature of presidential travel at the turn of the twenty-first century: Nixon had gone to China in 1972 with about three hundred people, his official party numbering a mere thirty-four, accompanied by a press corps of some eighty-seven reporters. To be fair, defenders of Clinton observed, the Nixon trip was the inaugural journey to China, one undertaken to establish diplomatic ties with the communist regime. Clinton, flying to China a generation later, came with a vast economic and strategic agenda, which dictated a proportional increase in the size of the delegation. Also, the Nixon visit to China had taken place in a context of Cold War suspicions, at a time when the Chinese authorities severely curtailed the size of the presidential entourage; Clinton visited the nation in an altered climate of relative openness.

Most Americans viewed such presidential travel abroad largely in terms of Air Force One, seeing the storied plane not narrowly as a mode of transport but as a symbol of the United States on Chinese soil. Less apparent to those who followed the Clinton trip to China was the fact that the Clinton entourage required several large C-141 air force transports, carrying among other things sixty tons of equipment, ten armored limousines, and two "road runners," the black vans filled with communications equipment. Small details also dictated the precise contents of presidential luggage, from bottled water for the president and first lady to the "blue goose," the bulletproof lectern always in readiness for a presidential speech. Space was allocated as well for certain special personnel, including a valet for the president and a hairdresser for First Lady Hillary Rodham Clinton, and for a coterie of secretaries, speechwriters, doctors, and photographers.[7]

During Clinton's tenure in office there was a rare mishap associated with the operation of Air Force One, an incident that showcased the high expectations routinely associated with presidential travel. In January 1998, Clinton had flown on a presidential 707 to Champaign, Illinois, for a speech at the University of Illinois, part of an itinerary that took the president across the Midwest. Once the speech was completed, Clinton promptly made his way back to the airport to board Air Force One for the next leg of his whirlwind trip. While the presidential plane taxied to the runway for takeoff, the landing gear slipped off the taxiway into a patch of damp earth. Onlookers were shocked to see Air Force One mired in the muck. The cockpit crew prudently opted not to attempt any extraordinary measure to free the mired plane, and a backup plane had to be flown to Champaign to pick up the president. During the long delay, as local and federal security officials arranged for the backup plane, Clinton passed the time playing cards with staff members.

In the aftermath of the incident, the flight crew was reassigned to other flying duties. The high standards of the 89th Airlift Wing did not tolerate such mishaps, no matter how minor in character.[8] The Clinton years were remembered as a time when Air Force One became a regular and highly visible extension of the White House, a reflection of the altered nature of the modern American presidency.

George W. Bush

George W. Bush came to the White House after winning a narrow victory in the electoral college in the hotly contested 2000 presidential election. A former governor of

Texas, Bush assumed the highest office in the land at the dawn of a new century. When he took up residence at 1600 Pennsylvania Avenue, the new president could not have anticipated that he and the country would soon face an unprecedented national crisis. On Tuesday, September 11, 2001, terrorists crashed hijacked airliners into the World Trade Center towers in New York City and the Pentagon in Washington, D.C. As events unfolded that day, Air Force One became a centerpiece in this national emergency. As an airborne extension of the White House, the plane gave the president instant mobility and a platform from which to respond to an extraordinary challenge to the United States. But in the stress of the crisis, Air Force One's state-of-the-art communications systems — even with all its technical sophistication — proved vulnerable to occasional breakdowns.

En route from Columbus, Ohio, to St. Louis, Missouri, President George W. Bush talks to members of his staff in a passageway of Air Force One on February 20, 2001.

"It was like a rocket. For a good ten minutes, the plane was going almost straight up." Dan Bartlett, White House communications director

On September 11, 2001, terrorists hijacked commercial airliners and flew them into the twin towers of the World Trade Center (*left*) and the Pentagon in Washington (*center*). At right, President Bush learns details of the terrorist attacks by telephone in a classroom at the Emma E. Booker Elementary School in Sarasota, Florida. Director of communications Dan Bartlett points to television coverage of the event. Also pictured are Deborah Loewer (behind Bush), director of the White House situation room, and senior advisor Karl Rove (*right*).

President Bush had flown on Air Force One to Bradenton International Airport in Sarasota, Florida, on Monday, September 10, staying overnight at special lodgings at Longboat Key. The following morning, at about 8:00 A.M., Bush and his entourage made their way to the nearby Emma E. Booker Elementary School, where the president sought to promote his education program with a visit to a second-grade class.

Shortly after his arrival at the school, President Bush received word of the terrorist attacks. The inferno enveloping the World Trade Center towers suggested a coordinated plot, but there was an initial uncertainty as to the identity of the terrorists or their plans for further attacks. The terrorist assault was sudden and inexplicable to Americans, who crowded around their television sets to watch the drama unfold.

Retreating to a separate classroom where the Secret Service, following established procedure, had set up a secure telephone link to the White House, the president talked with Vice President Richard Cheney and National Security Adviser Dr. Condoleezza Rice at about 9:30 A.M. At the White House, Cheney had been rushed to an underground bunker, the Presidential Emergency Operations Center, where Rice and others began to implement the established contingency plan for a national emergency. The Secret Service moved promptly to ensure presidential succession, shielding no less than fifteen people who were in line to become president in the event that Bush and Cheney were killed.

President Bush opted to move to Air Force One as soon as possible. At the moment Bush's limousine and entourage of escort vehicles sped toward the Bradenton airport, a third hijacked airliner crashed into the Pentagon. The familiar symbol of American military power endured a violent explosion, followed by a raging fire and a billowing plume of dark smoke rising above the Potomac River. It was at this moment that word reached the White House staff to evacuate. Yet another hijacked airliner, on a shadowy flight path and still unaccounted for, might be en route to Washington for a fiery crash into the Capitol or perhaps the White House itself.

Along with most Americans, President Bush watched video footage of the hijacked airliners crashing into the World Trade Center towers with disbelief; he was slow to comprehend fully the scale and audacity of the terrorist attack. "I thought it was an accident," he later mused. "I thought it was a pilot error. I thought some foolish soul had gotten lost — and made a terrible mistake."[9]

Offutt AFB
Bellevue, NE

Barksdale AFB
Shreveport, LA

Andrews AFB
Camp Springs, MD

Sarasota, Florida

Source: CBSNews.com

Bush's advisers strongly urged him to fly out of Bradenton immediately, fearing that the presidential 747 might be on the target list of the terrorists. Just before 10:00 A.M., Air Force One lifted off the runway, taking a steep ascent into the morning sky over Sarasota. Bush's pilot, Colonel Mark Tillman, maintained this steep angle for nearly ten minutes until the plane reached altitude. In the chaos of the moment, many rumors swept over the land, including that Camp David had been hit and that the Bush ranch in Texas was in the cross hairs for yet another attack. Coinciding with this moment, the first of the twin towers collapsed in an avalanche of concrete, dust, glass, and human bodies. Within thirty minutes, the second tower fell.[10]

On Air Force One, now flying at an altitude well above commercial air traffic, security considerations dominated the thoughts and actions of Colonel Tillman and the Secret Service agents aboard. A guard was placed at the door of the cockpit, the passenger manifest was checked and checked again, and the crew reviewed the emergency evacuation plan. Air Force One's radio contact with air traffic control was not conducted through routine channels. Tillman opted to use a telephone link to avoid any possible monitoring by terrorists: "We didn't tell them our destination or what directions we were heading," he later observed. "We basically just talked to them and said, 'OK, fine, we have no clearance at this time; we are just going to fly across the United States.'"[11] The decision had been made, at the urging of the Secret Service and with the reluctant approval of the president, not to fly directly to Washington.

Below, left: Secret Service agents and military police go on high alert with the September 11 national emergency, requiring all passengers on Air Force One to undergo a thorough check and screening.
Center: While en route to Shreveport, Louisiana, on September 11, President Bush and his staff look out the window at their F-16 escort.
Right: Air Force One sits on the tarmac at Barksdale Air Force Base, near Shreveport on September 11. An armed guard signals the tight security surrounding the president's movements on that fateful day.

"We basically just talked to them and said, 'OK, fine...we are jus

A dramatic scene unfolds above America's heartland as a U.S. Air Force F-16 flies escort for Air Force One on the presidential plane's final leg home to Washington, D.C., on September 11. The president flew to Barksdale Air Force Base in Louisiana and Offutt Air Force Base in Nebraska before returning to the nation's capital.

going to fly across the United States.'" Col. Mark Tillman, pilot

⑥

This decision set the stage for Air Force One to make two separate landings before getting the green light to head home, first at Barksdale Air Force Base in Louisiana and then at Offutt Air Force Base in Nebraska. While en route to Louisiana, two F-16 fighters of the Texas Air National Guard rose to provide escort for the presidential plane. The fighters established an eighty-mile protective zone around Air Force One, preparing to investigate any wayward aircraft that might enter this air space.

Security advisers to the president had advocated extreme caution in the face of the sudden terrorist attack. During the morning hours of September 11, at the most chaotic time in the crisis, the White House grappled with the imperative to provide for the safety of the president and then to reassure a stunned public that Washington was indeed gaining mastery over the extraordinary situation. For Bush, the delays were difficult to endure; he became increasingly restive with his zigzagging itinerary through the Midwest. He wished to return to Washington as soon as possible.

While in flight on Air Force One, President Bush discovered that he could not make optimal use of the high-tech communications system on the plane or even monitor real-time news coverage on television.[12] The president was

④

⑤

How the Other Leaders Fly

Many Heads of State Have Their Own "Air Force One"

The advent of the airplane radically transformed the mode of travel for heads of state, a process that began slowly in the 1930s and gained considerable momentum in the jet age. Today, most political leaders, from the smallest nations to the major powers of the world, rich or poor, routinely fly as part of their official duties. Some nations have organized special air units for executive travel. While Air Force One operations have established a world standard for luxury and technical sophistication, the Americans are not alone.

The Japanese, in fact, use a more advanced version of the Boeing 747-200s now in American presidential service, having purchased two high-tech 747-400s. These variants of the Boeing 747 are recognizable by their winglets and extended upper decks. The government of Japan obtained these state-of-the-art jumbo jet transports in 1991 for the use of the prime minister and other high-ranking officials. While dedicated to executive air travel, the Japanese jets are tagged for special duties such as emergency airlift of Japanese nationals living abroad, international emergency relief flights, and support of United Nations activities. The jets are maintained by the Special Airlift Group of Japan's Air Self-Defense Force at Chitose Air Base.

The Japanese configuration of the Boeing 747-400 jumbo jets mirrors in many ways the American model. Each plane is identical in its interior configuration, including an office compartment for the prime minister, a conference room, and accommodations for the press. One interesting facet of Japanese operations, however, is the requirement that a highly trained maintenance

Japan's Emperor Akihito and Empress Michiko wave as they disembark from their government plane at Prague on July 6, 2002.

staff fly on board the executive jet transport on all official trips.[13]

With the debut of the twenty-first century, Russia — reflecting a new leadership and political system — has inaugurated its own version of Air Force One. Vladimir Putin, president of the Russian Federation, has expressed a keen interest in the construction of his "airborne office," a variant of the Ilyushin Il-96-300 transport. The presidential plane has been a major project for the Ilyushin aviation workers at Voronezh, a well-known center for aircraft construction in Russia.

Following tradition, Moscow has placed a shroud of state secrecy around the Voronezh project. However, scattered reports on the Russian presidential plane suggest that the interior design will be highly modern, but not necessarily luxurious in its appointments — no gold leaf décor or rich adornment. The final configuration, following standard practice, will include offices, conference rooms, galleys, and comfortable seating. Interestingly, the presidential plane — with the inscription *Rossiya* (Russia) prominently displayed on the fuselage — will contain high-tech security systems, rumored to include a special escape capsule for the Russian president.[14]

The German version of Air Force One, known as the "Flying Chancellor's Office," is a white-painted Airbus A310. The plane is attached to the German Air Force, as suggested by the name *Luftwaffe* and the black iron cross insignia emblazoned on the forward fuselage. Heiko Stolzke, writing about this flagship of the *Luftwaffe,* has described it as a "comfortable cross between a hotel and a mobile home," adding that anyone anticipating that the plane possesses the "oriental luxury of James Bond gadgetry" will be disappointed.[15] The *Luftwaffe* A310 provides a comfortable setting for official travel, but in no way approaches the American Air Force One in design or technical sophistication. The spartan design includes essential features such as offices, conference rooms, and galleys. For the chancellor, the plane offers only two comfortable berths and a small bathroom. One important feature aboard, though, is the placement of a special communications center for the use of the chancellor on all official trips.

British prime minister Tony Blair travels often, and he routinely makes use of chartered British Airways jets for his overseas trips. On occasion, he has used British Airways supersonic Concorde aircraft for transatlantic flights to Washington. As the Concorde is gradually phased out of active

service on British Airways, the prime minister's office will continue to charter commercial jets. Typically, Blair has chartered a British Airways Boeing 777 for his travel, which will no doubt be the preferred mode of transport in the future.

The list of other nations with special executive aircraft is a long one, from the relatively modest A319CJ serving the president of Venezuela to the richly appointed 747 jumbo jet dedicated for the exclusive use of the Saudi king and royal family. Whatever the size of the plane or the nature of its special interior appointments, the use of Air Force One–type aircraft has become a familiar dimension of world politics in the twenty-first century.

Above, clockwise from top left: A Canadian honor guard joins the welcoming ceremonies for Japanese prime minister Junichiro Koizumi at Calgary, Alberta, on June 25, 2002, for the G8 economic summit; Russian Federation president Vladimir Putin and his wife depart France for home in his official plane; Putin often flies on Russia's huge Ilyushin Il-96-300 air transport, shown here after landing in Tokyo; Britain's prime minister Tony Blair takes notes during an official trip from London to Egypt on October 11, 2001; Blair chartered a British Airways Concorde for a trip to the United States on November 7, 2001.

"The Pearl Harbor of the 21st Century took place today. We think it is Osama bin Laden." George W. Bush

angered when his telephone link was severed in mid-sentence with Vice President Cheney. Bush shouted, "This is inexcusable; get me the Vice President."[16]

Only when Bush reached the underground communications facility of the U.S. Strategic Command Center at Offutt did he have a chance to conduct a teleconference with the White House, the Pentagon, the FBI, and the CIA. It was in this conference that CIA director George Tenet answered the president's question about who had launched the attacks: "Sir, I believe it's Al Qaeda. We're doing the assessment but it looks like, its feels like, it smells like Al Qaeda."[17]

President Bush stayed at the air force bunker in Nebraska briefly, working on an address he planned to deliver to the nation that night. He firmly indicated his decision to return to the White House. In the words of his press secretary, Ari Fleischer, "At one point, he said he didn't want any tinhorn terrorist keeping him out of Washington."[18]

The national emergency had unfolded in the capital in a peculiar way, against a backdrop of the terrorist attack on the Pentagon and fears that other Washington landmarks, including the White House, might be on the target list. Shortly after the terrorists crashed an airliner into the Pentagon, the White House had contacted Andrews Air Force Base with the instructions, "Get into the air, now!" This order went directly to the 121st Fighter Squadron of the District of Columbia Air National Guard.

How elements of the 121st Squadron responded to this urgent call became a testimony to the personal resourcefulness of air force pilots in the face of a national emergency. The White House had called for the mobilization of F-16 fighters at Andrews to provide air cover. These particular fighters were not on alert status on September 11 because their unit was not attached to the North American Aerospace Defense Command air defense network.

In reality, there were only three fighters available to fly sorties in defense of Washington. These fighters possessed minimal or no armament. One of the F-16s had no operable armament — no missiles and no ammunition for its 20-millimeter gun. The other two fighters were equipped only with a full load of nonlethal 20-millimeter training rounds.

With the Pentagon in flames, the three pilots of the 121st Fighter Squadron scrambled to meet any hijacked airliners on their way to Washington. The pilots agreed among themselves that — in the absence of any lethal weapons — they would ram any threatening aircraft entering the air space over the capital.

As the hours passed, steps were taken to provide adequate fighter escort for Air Force One when it entered the airspace over Washington. Late in the day on September 11, the fighter presence over Washington had been augmented with fighters drawn from other units on the East Coast. By this time, too, the F-16s flown by the 121st pilots were properly armed with AIM-9 missiles, and they were folded into the escort group.

When Air Force One left Offutt Air Force Base for the final leg home, a flight of F-16s from Ellington Air Force Base in Texas brought up the rear. When the presidential plane made its approach to Andrews, nine hours had passed since Bush had learned of the attack on the twin towers in New York City. The dramatic landing of Air Force One was heralded by a clearing pass by one of the 121st F-16s; as the president's plane taxied to a stop, the escort fighters circled above to provide protective cover.[19]

Upon reaching the White House, the president dictated a simple statement for the daily log at the conclusion of the long day: "The Pearl Harbor of the 21st Century took place today. We think it is Osama bin Laden." The president had alerted the nation to the actual clandestine group responsible for terrorism.[20]

No sooner had Air Force One landed than a debate

President George W. Bush, *opposite,* **disembarks from Marine One at Andrews Air Force Base on September 14, 2001, to board Air Force One,** *below,* **for his historic visit to New York City after the terrorist attacks on the World Trade Center.**

arose over whether, in fact, there had been a threat to the presidential plane. The claim had been made that a threat to Air Force One reached the White House on the day of the terrorist attack. News reports, however, challenged this notion, suggesting the call had never been made to the White House. Fleischer indicated that such a call had been made, but the press secretary later appeared to back off from the claim. Vice President Cheney initially maintained the posture that a credible threat had been received, and this threat was taken seriously in the context of the White House response to the crisis. Subsequently, however, he qualified his position, admitting that the alarm may have been a bogus one.[21]

The whole debate over the real or imagined threat to Air Force One dovetailed into the larger controversy over the president's decision not to fly directly back to Washington on September 11. The delays and the peculiar flight path of Air Force One had reflected the extraordinary

Life on George W. Bush's Air Force One

Bush Is a "Frequent Flyer" as Presidential Air Travel Enters the Twenty-First Century

When George W. Bush became the 43rd president of the United States in January 2001, he could not have realized that his tenure in office would be an occasion for a remarkable new chapter in the history of Air Force One. Faced with terrorist attacks on New York City and Washington, D.C., on September 11, 2001, Bush mobilized the presidential plane as his communications center during the national emergency. The reality of Air Force One as an extension of the Oval Office became apparent once again during the anxious hours of that fateful day.

On more routine flights, Air Force One has offered President Bush a comfortable means to reach any domestic or foreign destination. Following tradition, Bush has forged his own approach to the presidential plane. The chief executive's compartment on Air Force One, situated in the forward nose section, provides a sequestered precinct for relaxation or work. Often garbed in his lightweight blue jacket emblazoned with the words Air Force One, Bush moves about freely on the plane, holds meetings in his personal compartment, or chats with the crew and the invited guests on board. Unlike his father, the younger Bush rarely ventures into the press corps compartment, preferring to keep his contact with the reporters minimal. Also, in contrast to his immediate predecessor, Bill Clinton, Bush has severely restricted the number of people in his official party on any presidential trip — no huge entourages on foreign treks. The Bush Air Force One exudes a mood of simplicity, restraint, and discipline.

For passengers on Air Force One, there are numerous televisions on board to watch the news

or to take in a movie on a long flight. Bush takes pains to supply his guests and crew with baskets of candy and fresh fruit. For Bush, there is the option of making phone calls to friends, colleagues, and celebrities on the ground. In 2002, for example, the president made congratulatory telephone calls to Emmitt Smith, the running back for the Dallas Cowboys, for breaking the National Football League's rushing record, and to Jackie Autry, widow of the former owner of the Anaheim Angels, on the team's winning the World Series.[22]

Taking note of their boss's interest in baseball

Left: The president and first lady arrive at MacDill Air Force Base in Tampa, Florida, on March 26, 2003. Lower left: Barney, one of the Bushes' dogs, requires some coaxing before boarding Air Force One at Andrews Air Force Base on August 6, 2002. Lower right: Sporting an Air Force One jacket, President Bush prepares for his meeting with Chinese President Jiang Zemin on his flight from South Korea to Beijing on February 21, 2002.

as a former co-owner of the Texas Rangers, the White House staff provides videotaped Rangers games for the president's casual viewing while on Air Force One. When not watching baseball, Bush is an avid viewer of war movies, a practice that gained considerable momentum after the September 11 national crisis.[23]

Bush appreciates Air Force One for its unrivaled role as a symbol of the American presidency, something his father and Bill Clinton fully exploited in the promotion of their domestic programs.[24] These presidents routinely combined

The president and first lady share a desk on board Air Force One during a flight to Elmendorf Air Force Base, near Anchorage, Alaska, on February 16, 2002.

policy events with political events, making full use of Air Force One as an effective arm of the White House. Joining the president on Air Force One provides a political candidate with instant stature in any election year. President Bush made extensive use of Air Force One in the 2002 election cycle, as did Bill Clinton during his two terms in the 1990s.

While flying on Air Force One, Bush always takes time for exercise, a way to vary the normal routine of reading briefing papers, working on speeches, and conferring with aides. On long trips, the president has made extensive use of a tread-mill, which can be set up in the plane's conference room. Bush and his staff follow a precise discipline of naps and exercise to avoid jet lag on extended flights. Typically, Bush prefers to depart from foreign destinations in the evening, so he can arrive home at a civilized hour, to allow for a full night's rest before resuming his duties at the White House the next day.[25]

President Bush — as with his predecessors — has sovereignty over the flight's menu. If his father garnered some fame for banning broccoli from Air Force One, the son has been noted for a preference for egg salad sandwiches on toast. For passengers on the presidential plane, the daily menu appears on gold-edged menu cards. Most who have eaten on Air Force One report that the fare is more than adequate, but not as luxurious as some might imagine.[26] For modern-day presidents, Air Force One remains an awe-inspiring mode of transport, a place for work and policy-making, and a sanctuary in times of crisis.

"Air Force One epitomizes the strength and majesty of the United States of America." George H. W. Bush

context of the day, a moment in time that the president himself described as the "fog" of war.

The phrase "homeland security" soon entered the American political lexicon, the conjunction of these two words reflecting the new collective sense of national vulnerability in the aftermath of September 11. The phrase gained immediate and widespread currency, eventually becoming the name for a new cabinet-level department with the mandate to combat terrorism in the United States.

Air Force One had played a highly visible role in what the German magazine *Der Spiegel* described as "the most perfect act of terror in history."[27] Not since the assassination of John F. Kennedy had Air Force One been center stage in a national tragedy. Like Pearl Harbor, the stunning events of September 11 became fixed in the nation's collective memory, giving way to a determination to strike back against the perceived threats — in Afghanistan, Iraq, and beyond. Once again, Air Force One became part of the equation, as in the case of the second Gulf War of 2003, when President Bush flew on the plane to wartime plan-

Members of the deck crew look on as President George W. Bush lands in an S-3 Viking (Navy One) on the USS *Abraham Lincoln* on May 1, 2003. Bush's landing on the carrier established a first in the history of presidential air travel.

ning conferences in the Azores and Northern Ireland with Coalition partner British prime minister Tony Blair. As in earlier decades, the presidential plane had been mobilized to play a key role in a national emergency.

The second Gulf War gave President Bush a rare opportunity to push the envelope in the saga of White House travel. On May 1, 2003, Bush flew on an S-3 Viking, a small fixed-wing navy jet, to the USS *Abraham Lincoln,* an aircraft carrier returning from the war. The S-3 Viking, dubbed "Navy One" because of its presidential passenger, took off for the short hop to the carrier from the North Island Naval Air Station in Coronado, California, just minutes before noon PST.

Bush sat in the co-pilot's position next to the navy pilot in command on the historic flight. As a polite bow to security concerns, a Secret Service agent sat behind the president. While en route to the carrier on the fifteen-minute jaunt, Bush — once a jet fighter pilot in the Texas Air National Guard — momentarily took the controls of the plane. The crew of the USS *Abraham Lincoln* and a stunned national television audience watched as Navy One, accompanied by a second S-3 Viking, made a dramatic flyover. As Navy One touched down, the carrier's arresting cables stretched across the deck caught Bush's plane and wrenched it to an abrupt stop within 400 feet.

Later that same night, President Bush addressed the nation from the deck of the USS *Abraham Lincoln* to announce the end of active military operations in the war. The televised events of that day on the carrier predictably prompted widespread praise for Bush, but the feat also received a measure of criticism in the press and in Congress. Had Bush displayed the adventuresome spirit of Teddy Roosevelt or merely mimicked the role of a "Top Gun" aviator for maximum political effect, as some of his critics complained? Whatever the flight's merits or justifications, Bush had clearly established a new milestone:

an unprecedented landing by a sitting president on an operational aircraft carrier.

The dramatic carrier landing stood in a long tradition of perceived risk-taking in presidential air travel. Perhaps Franklin D. Roosevelt prompted the most concern among his contemporaries over the inherent dangers of flying. Roosevelt's transatlantic flight on the *Dixie Clipper* in 1943 for the Casablanca conference during World War II represented a bold and, for some at the time, reckless undertaking. Roosevelt's subsequent flights to participate in Allied meetings at Tehran and Yalta only accentuated this criticism. Over time, many presidential trips, both domestic and foreign, have been challenged for their wisdom, practicality, or legitimacy.

President Bush's aerial spectacular came in the centennial year of flight. Among all the technological marvels that have shaped modern life, aviation arguably has been one of the most influential — and the airplane eventually became the optimal means of travel for occupants of the White House. No doubt President James Monroe, one of America's most determined travelers in the nineteenth century, would marvel at the global reach of his successors in the Air Age. Monroe's celebrated tours of the country in 1817 and 1819 took months to complete. The discomfort, fatigue, and isolation associated with Monroe's journeys — conducted without any entourage of security agents, aides, or reporters — reminds us of how the operations of Air Force One stand in sharp contrast to the glacial pace of presidential travel in earlier times.

The story of presidential travel, especially in the Air Age, reflects this new reality. Modern-day occupants of the White House enjoy the splendors of high-tech jumbo jets to reach their destinations, at home or abroad. Their travels are pursued in unparalleled comfort and safety. President Franklin Roosevelt's celebrated flight to the Casablanca conference in 1943 ushered in this new era of

Air Force One arrives at the San Jose del Cabo International Airport on the southern tip of Mexico's 1,000-mile-long Baja Peninsula on October 26, 2002. The plane's slick livery provides a dramatic contrast against the rugged desert mountains.

presidential air travel. One should note, however, that during his twelve years in office, FDR primarily traveled by train, accumulating by one reckoning some 544,000 miles on America's railroads.[28] FDR, in fact, had set the stage for a dramatic revolution in presidential travel. The story of Air Force One, in large measure, unfolded in the decades after Roosevelt's pioneering flight, when presidents gradually abandoned trains for the airplane. At the dawn of the twenty-first century, Air Force One has become an essential component in the conduct of foreign affairs and an awe-inspiring way to project presidential leadership at home.

The role of Air Force One in American life, however, cannot be understood solely in terms of its awe-inspiring capabilities as a mode of transport. The extraordinary plane — wherever it flies — embodies something larger and more intangible: the White House aloft, a powerful symbol of the American presidency, indeed the image of the United States itself.

Where Are They Now?

Historic Presidential Aircraft Find New Homes After Years of White House Service

The U.S. Air Force aircraft assigned to the presidential wing have acquired a unique cachet in the popular mind. Many of these historic planes are now housed in air museums and presidential libraries across the country. The passage from high-profile flights at Andrews Air Force Base to the serene, if static, environs of a museum exhibit is a logical sequence, although the script varies with each plane.

One of the most memorable retirements of an Air Force One aircraft came in 1998, when SAM 26000 flew to Dayton, Ohio, for public display in the U.S. Air Force Museum. This famed Boeing 707 had entered the presidential wing in 1962 and, in the course of its long service life of three and one half decades, had flown a total of seven presidents on myriad domestic and foreign trips.

SAM 26000, with its distinctive Raymond Loewy paint scheme, became an awe-inspiring image of Air Force One in the course of its long history. No other presidential plane could rival its historic flight log. This was the plane that had flown John F. Kennedy to Dallas, Texas, on November 22, 1963, only to return the assassinated president to Washington, D.C., the same fateful day. Americans retained vivid memories of SAM 26000 in Dallas: the crowded cabin serving as the locale for the swearing-in of Lyndon B. Johnson as president, and the rear compartment (with seats and part of the bulkhead removed) co-opted to transport the casket of the slain president home.

SAM 26000 played a highly visible role in the diplomatic history of the United States. In 1963, Kennedy flew on the plane to Berlin for one of the most memorable moments in the history of the Cold War, when he made his "Ich Bin Ein Berliner" speech. During the Nixon years, SAM 26000 was deployed for several special missions. Henry Kissinger flew on the plane to Paris in 1970 for his clandestine talks with the North Vietnamese. Two years later, SAM 26000 transported President Richard M. Nixon on his dramatic visit to China, setting the stage for a major transformation in international affairs. In 1981, President Ronald Reagan deployed the same plane to carry an official delegation of former presidents Nixon, Ford, and Carter to the funeral of slain president Anwar el-Sadat in Egypt.

A twin Boeing 707, SAM 27000 carved out its own remarkable record as a presidential plane, beginning its twenty-nine-year service in 1972. Replacing SAM 26000 as the primary presidential plane, it became the familiar transport for presidents Nixon, Ford, Carter, and Reagan, and later a back-up aircraft that would carry presidents George H. W. Bush, Clinton, and George W. Bush. As a former president, Jimmy Carter flew on SAM 27000 for his historic meeting with the newly released Iranian hostages in January 1981. The plane logged some 444 missions as Air Force One, not to mention its work as a VIP transport for vice presidents, cabinet secretaries, and other high-ranking officials — a total of one million miles.

As a presidential plane, SAM 27000 is perhaps best remembered for its historic flights during Ronald Reagan's two terms in the 1980s. Reagan accumulated some 211 trips on SAM 27000. He flew on the plane to Berlin in 1987 to make his Cold War challenge to Mikhail Gorbachev to "tear down" the Berlin Wall, and SAM 27000 became

the primary mode of transport for Reagan to attend conferences with his Soviet counterpart in Geneva, Reykjavik, and Moscow.

Given its historic ties to the Reagan administration, the plane was decommissioned and assigned to the Ronald Reagan Presidential Library on permanent loan. On August 29, 2001, George W. Bush took part in a celebratory flight on SAM 27000, flying from Waco to San Antonio, Texas, shortly before the plane made its final flight to California and into history. President Bush used the occasion to recognize the venerable place of the plane in the history of Air Force One.[29] Exhibit plans call for "Old 27000" to become the centerpiece for an exhibition on presidential travel at the Reagan Library, in Simi Valley, California, in late 2004.[30]

Other retired presidential aircraft are housed today in a variety of museums across the United

have served in an auxiliary role in the presidential wing include a Beech VC-6A, an Aero Commander U-4B, a North American T-39A Sabreliner, and a Lockheed VC-140B Jetstar.

The Pima Air & Space Museum proudly displays another presidential plane of note, the VC-118A *Liftmaster,* a military version of the DC-6B airliner. Painted in the distinctive blue and white livery of presidential aircraft, the Pima *Liftmaster* was the last presidential plane to be piston-powered. President Kennedy first used the plane in September 1961. It remained part of the presidential wing during the 1960s, ending its service with President Johnson. Another artifact from the Johnson era is the Pima Museum's Sikorsky H-34C Choctaw, an army helicopter with the distinctive white top associated with present-day presidential helicopters flown by the U.S. Marines.

No listing of presidential aircraft is complete without reference to SAM 970. This was the plane on which Eisenhower made the first presidential jet flight during his second term. SAM 970 possesses a venerable flight record, having served presidents Eisenhower, Kennedy, Johnson, and Nixon. The plane's passenger manifest also includes many flights by Henry Kissinger on his various diplomatic forays and even one flight with Soviet leader Nikita Khrushchev on board during his memorable visit to the United States in 1959. Today, SAM 970 is housed at the Museum of Flight in Seattle, Washington.

As Jerald terTorst once remarked, when the government retires its presidential planes, a piece of history is also retired. Yet, as artifacts, these extraordinary planes offer a dramatic way to chronicle presidential history.[32]

Opposite: Franklin Roosevelt's plane, the *Sacred Cow, top,* and Truman's plane, the *Independence, bottom,* are on exhibit at the U.S. Air Force Museum in Dayton, Ohio. *Above:* SAM 970, which served from Eisenhower to Reagan, is on display at Boeing Field in Seattle.

States. The U.S. Air Force Museum in Dayton, Ohio, claims the most surviving presidential planes. In addition to SAM 26000, among its ensemble of historic aircraft is the first transport assigned to White House service, the Douglas VC-54C, the fabled *Sacred Cow* that flew Franklin Delano Roosevelt to his World War II meetings with allies Winston Churchill and Joseph Stalin. The *Sacred Cow* is preserved today with the special lift designed for the partially paralyzed Roosevelt to board and exit his plane while in a wheelchair.

The rich collection at the Air Force Museum also includes Harry S. Truman's Douglas VC-118 *Independence,* with its distinctive livery mimicking a bird in flight. Another presidential plane from the formative era is Dwight D. Eisenhower's stunning Lockheed VC-121E *Columbine III.* The Eisenhower plane is a variant of the "Super Connie," arguably the most beautiful multi-engine piston-powered plane in history. When these pioneer aircraft are displayed in proximity to SAM 26000, one can trace the history of presidential air travel from World War II to the late 1990s in one hangar.[31]

While the Air Force Museum showcases the major presidential planes, there are other, lesser known aircraft that served American presidents, including the Bell UH-13J helicopter that established an important milestone by taking President Eisenhower aloft, a first in the history of vertical flight. Other memorable aircraft on exhibit that

Acknowledgments

THIS ILLUSTRATED HISTORY of presidential air travel drew upon the talents and labors of a large group of people — historians, archivists, researchers, editors, photographers, museum curators, Air Force personnel, and newsmen. While it aims to be comprehensive in its coverage, looking at the entire phenomenon of presidential travel and Air Force One, this book possesses only a momentary grasp on a story that will continue to unfold in the twenty-first century.

As the author, I wish to express my profound appreciation for the wisdom, tireless energy, and expertise of my friend and colleague Gene Eisman, who served as the researcher and consulting editor for the book. Gene helped to fashion the concept of the book, generated a vast array of primary and secondary sources, read and commented on all the draft chapters and sidebars, and prepared the annotated bibliography. He was a creative and essential force behind the book.

A number of people made valued contributions to the research for the book. Sergeant Kirk Clear, historian of the 89th Airlift Wing at Andrews Air Force Base, opened many doors to us and provided welcome support in our quest for documentary and photographic resources. Lieutenant Colonel Everett Dewolfe, president of the SAM FOX Association (presidential air crew alumni), pointed us, in a very timely way, to many individuals with special knowledge of the history of Air Force One. Among them, we wish to express our profound appreciation to Joe Chappell, who offered many insights into the operations of the presidential air wing in the 1960s and 1970s.

Others contributed welcome insights and historical materials. Dan Preston, editor of the James Monroe Papers, provided us with some fascinating, still largely unknown, materials on the remarkable travels of James Monroe, who was single-handedly responsible for ending the cloistered existence of presidents in the formative years of the republic. Glen Sweeting and Lawrence DiRicco assisted in many ways on selected topics. And Robert J. Ribando of the University of Virginia's School of Engineering and Applied Sciences provided us with some interesting articles from *Forbes FYI*.

Two newsmen, Bob Schieffer and Robert Pierpoint, shared with us their insider's perspective on the story of Air Force One, in Pierpoint's case going back to the Eisenhower years. I appreciate their willingness to share insights and anecdotes with us on presidential air travel over the years.

I wish to express my deep appreciation to my editor, Garrett Brown, at Tehabi Books. His keen enthusiasm for the topic, his editorial skills, and his impressive patience made the whole enterprise thoroughly enjoyable. John Baxter, senior art director, played a major role in shaping the layout of the book, being responsible for the elegant design and outstanding graphics. I appreciate as well the professionalism and hard work of Mark Santos and his tenacious assistant, Mary Beth Farlow, in leading the effort to identify the many photographs and illustrations for the project. Marty Remmell and Katie Franco also provided timely and able assistance throughout the project as part of the talented team at Tehabi Books.

Finally, I wish to thank my wife, Patricia, for her constancy and support and for her timely, if informal, role as a reader and editor of early drafts of the chapters.

Further Reading
by Gene Eisman

Although U.S. presidents have obviously traveled to some degree since the advent of the office, the list of books and other materials chronicling those trips is not a long one. What does exist is best categorized by division into a historical overview of presidential travel followed by a discussion of books, documentaries, Web sites, and even some novels about Air Force One. This list is by definition selective, aimed at getting the inquisitive reader or viewer started on the road to greater knowledge, rather than offering a full list of destinations.

I. Books

A. HISTORICAL BACKGROUND

Monroe, James. *The Papers of James Monroe: A Documentary History of the Presidential Tours of James Monroe, 1817, 1818, 1819.* Vol. 1. Edited by Daniel Preston and Marlena C. DeLong. Westport, Conn.: Greenwood Press, 2003. A fascinating and detailed account of two major trips (1817 and 1819) by the fifth president, whose extended journeys to the northern and southern states and territories were the first of their kind by an American president. Monroe paid for the trips from his own assets and bank loans, since Congress provided only a salary, with no expenses.

Siuru, William D., Jr. *Presidential Cars & Transportation: From Horse and Carriage to Air Force One, the Story of How the Presidents of the United States Travel.* Iola, Wis.: Krause Publications, 1995. A comprehensive look at how U.S. presidents have traveled, ranging from horse-drawn carriages through the early automobile, to trains, and then planes. Well illustrated with photos of presidential limousines, private rail passenger cars, and aircraft.

Smith, A. Merriman. *Merriman Smith's Book of Presidents: A White House Memoir.* Edited by Timothy G. Smith. New York: W.W. Norton, 1972. The legendary United Press White House correspondent who covered presidents from FDR to Nixon offers his unique perspective on everything from FDR's slow train trips across America to Dallas on November 22, 1963. Little of note or interest about the presidents he covered eluded Smith's sharp reportorial eye, and he made the most of his extraordinary access to the chief executives.

Reilly, Michael F. *Reilly of the White House.* New York: Simon and Schuster, 1947. Reilly, head of FDR's Secret Service detail, provides an intimate and detailed look at life with the president, including planning, advancing and executing his aerial and rail journeys. Particularly detailed on the historic Casablanca, Cairo/Tehran, and Yalta summits. Reilly deals candidly with FDR's infirmities, including the president's realization that his partial paralysis from polio made him totally dependent on others for escape in event of a plane crash, fire, or other disaster. A true gem of presidential literature.

B. AIR FORCE ONE

Dorr, Robert F. *Air Force One.* St. Paul: MBI Publishing Company, 2002. A veteran and well-respected aviation history writer, Dorr delivers a volume heavy on photos and details of the various Air Force Ones, but light on the historical events directly connected to the presidents' flights. He notes that, before September 11, "Air Force One was becoming a little more accessible to press and public, and outsiders were being permitted to see a little of the plane's interior. Afterward, new security measures took hold." A significant shortcoming is the lack of footnotes and a bibliography.

Holder, Bill. *Planes of the Presidents.* Atglen, Penn.: Schiffer Publishing Ltd., 2000. This fifty-page volume offers a decent compilation of the various aircraft, large and small, used by presidents, but its usefulness is limited by an apparent lack of editing in the form of typos and some factual errors. Good photographic coverage of the lesser-known aircraft used occasionally by presidents.

Mikesh, Robert C. "Presidential Aircraft." *American Aviation Historical Society Journal,* 8, no. 2 (1963): 79–96. A pioneering effort by Mikesh, now a retired National Air & Space Museum senior curator, to chronicle and illustrate the history of presidential aircraft to 1963. Hard to find, but worth the effort, Mikesh's work stands the test of time.

terHorst, J. F. and Col. Ralph Albertazzie. *The Flying White House: The Story of Air Force One.* New York: Coward, McCann &

Geoghegan, Inc., 1979. The Rosetta Stone of all books on presidential flight; an essential starting point. Written by President Nixon's pilot and President Ford's first White House press secretary, it provides, among much else, a complete roster of presidential pilots from FDR to Carter; a detailed account of Nixon's "final flight" home in 1974; and Henry Kissinger's use of the president's plane to start the Paris peace talks with the North Vietnamese and to arrange Nixon's historic China journey. A drawback is that its coverage ends in 1979.

Walsh, Kenneth T. *Air Force One: A History of the Presidents and Their Planes.* New York: Hyperion, 2003. Walsh, *U.S. News and World Report*'s White House correspondent, is a veteran of some 200 flights on Air Force One. He has delivered a book long on gossip about its presidential passengers and somewhat short on the history of the plane itself. Walsh provides many anecdotes, some of them bizarre, on presidential behavior aloft, an approach that de-emphasizes the technical and operational dimensions of the Air Force One story.

C. Air Force One in Fiction

Corley, Edwin. *Air Force One: A Novel.* Garden City, N.Y.: Doubleday & Company, Inc., 1978. The author delivers an interest-ing pastiche of a book, mixing factual information on the operations of the real Air Force One, including LBJ's fabled round-the-world trip in 1967, with a wholly fictional plot about an attempt to shoot down the president's plane in Montana in the 1970s. The would-be aerial assassin's weapon of choice is a WW II-vintage P-38 fighter!

Denis, John. *Alistair MacLean's Air Force One Is Down.* New York: Fawcett Crest, 1981. This novel represented a not-very-subtle attempt to "franchise" MacLean's name by having another writer do a novel based on "a story outline" by the best-selling MacLean. This paperback's cover, showing Air Force One going down in flames in mountainous terrain, leaves little to the imagination. The plot, such as it is, revolves around an attempt by international criminals to use the *doppelganger* of a high-level air force security official to gain access to, and destroy, Air Force One.

Serling, Robert. *The President's Plane Is Missing.* Garden City, N.Y.: Doubleday & Company, Inc., 1967. The president's plane disappears from radar and its wreckage is located in Arizona. The real problems start when President Jeremy Haines' remains are not found at the crash scene; the plot becomes more complex by the page as reporters from a fictional news service seek to discover the true story. A made-for-television movie based on the novel in the early 1970s was a precursor of the 1997 film *Air Force One,* starring Harrison Ford.

———. *Air Force One Is Haunted.* New York: St. Martin's/Marek, 1985. In this highly creative work, the "ghost" of FDR visits the fictional President Jeremy Haines on board Air Force One, freely dispensing political advice and commentary to his "successor." In the end, Haines tests a new American anti-missile system that results in Russia abandoning all plans for world conquest and seeking peace with the U.S. In his book *President Reagan: The Role of a Lifetime,* Lou Cannon wrote that Reagan read Serling's novel while in office and that White House aides worried that public disclosure of that information would raise "troubling questions" in the press.

II. Documentaries

Air Force One, Flight II — The Planes and Their Presidents, 1991, Elliott Sluhan Productions, 90 minutes. Hosted and narrated by Charlton Heston. Interviews with Air Force One pilots and crews back to Truman and Eisenhower; Henry Kissinger on his use of the plane; and recollections of JFK, LBJ, and other presidents on Air Force One by reporters who flew with them.

Discovery Channel's Inside Air Force One, 1999, 60 minutes; produced for Discovery by ABC News. Good graphics showing the interior layout of the current Air Force One, along with a video tour of the plane's interior (also included in the other DVDs/videos).

National Geographic's Air Force One, 2001, 60 minutes. Spectacular footage of both presidential 747s in their huge hangar at Andrews Air Force Base. Interviews with four presidents, including George W. Bush, about life on Air Force One. The cameras follow President Clinton on a cross-country trip, showing how a president uses his time aboard for work and relaxation.

III. Web Sites

http://home.rose.net/~dingdong/
This self-styled, independent site provides well-illustrated histories of presidential planes and helicopters from the earliest days to the present.

http://www.boeing.com/defense-space/military/af1/flash.html
Boeing's own Air Force One site offers a fact sheet, technical specifications, and some additional information on the presidential

747s. Interestingly, a number of photographs showing the interior of the plane and other features were removed after September 11, 2001.

http://www.cbsnews.com/stories/2002/09/11/60II/main521718.shtml
On-line version of a CBS News show that aired on the first anniversary of the September 11 terrorist attacks. Includes video, text, and graphics, interviews with George H. Bush and Air Force One's pilot on September 11, interior footage of the plane and more.

http://www.cbsnews.com/stories/2002/9/18/earlyshow/living/travel/main522391.shtml
An excellent overview of the history of presidential helicopter use, complete with video.

http://www.museumofflight.org/
SAM 970, the VC-137 on which Eisenhower made the first-ever presidential jet flight in 1959, is on display at Seattle's Museum of Flight.

http://www.people.virginia.edu/~rjr/whdays/
A University of Virginia professor who served with the 89th Airlift Wing in the early 1970s pays tribute to all the presidents' airplanes on this superb site, complete with photos and a first-rate narrative.

http://www.pimaair.org/
The Pima Air & Space Museum in Tucson, Arizona, houses a VC-118A piston-engine transport used by JFK and a Sikorsky H-34C helicopter that was part of the presidential fleet during LBJ's administration.

http://www.reaganfoundation.org/airforceone/airforceone.asp
SAM 27000, which carried President Reagan on more than 200 presidential flights, will be displayed at the Ronald Reagan Presidential Library & Museum in Simi Valley, California, beginning in 2004. The story of the airplane and how it will be shown at the museum is detailed on this site.

http://www.wpafb.af.mil/museum/annex/ans.htm
The largest group of former presidential aircraft (nine) is on display at the United States Air Force Museum in Dayton, Ohio. This excellent site provides photographs and histories of the entire collection.

Notes

Introduction

1. Hugh Sidey, "The Loftiest Chariot," *Time,* July 7, 1986, p. 25. The source of Sidey's quotation may be found in Edward Gibbon's *History of the Decline and Fall of the Roman Empire,* vol. 3, chapter 31. Gibbon made extensive use of Ammianus's history, even recasting the Roman historian's words for greater clarity and style.

2. George H. W. Bush, "Man, Oh Man, Was It Comfortable," *Forbes FYI,* Winter 1996, p. 120.

Chapter 1

1. David McCullough, *John Adams* (New York: Simon and Schuster, 2001), p. 74.

2. Ibid., p. 74.

3. Quoted in Lucia S. Staunton and Kristin Onuf, Monticello Research Department, 1992, from "Jefferson's Journey to Washington," November 1800.

4. This section is based on Daniel Preston and Marlina DeLong, editors, *A Documentary History of the Presidential Tour of James Monroe, 1817, 1818, 1919,* vol. 1 (Westport, Conn.: Greenwood Publishing, 2003).

5. Allen Weinstein and David Rubel, *The Story of America: Freedom and Crisis from Settlement to Super Power* (New York: DK Publishers, 2002), p. 159.

6. David Herbert Donald, *Lincoln* (New York: Simon & Schuster, 1995), p. 547.

7. Walt Whitman, *Prose Works* (Philadelphia: David McKay, 1892; Bartleby.com, 2000), p. 45. See www.bartleby.com/229/

8. Ibid., p. 576.

9. Donald, p. 576.

10. William D. Siuru and Andrea Stewart, *Presidential Cars and Transportation: From Horse and Carriage to Air Force One, the Story of How Presidents of the United States Travel* (Iola, Wisc.: Krause Publications, 1995), pp. 16–19.

11. Ibid., p. 25.

Chapter 2

1. Veronica Gillespie, "T.R. on Film: The Theodore Roosevelt Association Collection at the Library of Congress," American Memory, Library of Congress.

See http://hdl.loc.gov/loc.mbrsmi/trmp.4087

2. *Aero* magazine, October 15, 1910, quoted in Jerald F. terHorst and Ralph Albertazzie, *The Flying White House* (New York: Coward, McCann and Geoghegan, 1979), p. 332.

3. Merriman Smith, *Merriman Smith's Book of Presidents: A White House Memoir,* edited by Timothy G. Smith (New York: W. W. Norton & Company, 1972), p. 155.

4. Robert C. Mikesh, "Presidential Aircraft," *American Aviation Historical Society Journal,* vol. 8, no. 2 (1963), pp. 79–96.

5. Doris Kearns Goodwin, *No Ordinary Time, Franklin and Eleanor Roosevelt: The Home Front in World War II* (New York: Simon & Schuster, 1994), p. 401.

6. Robert E. Sherwood, *Roosevelt and Hopkins, An Intimate History* (New York: Harper and Brothers, 1948), p. 67.

7. R. E. G. Davies, *Pan Am, An Airline and Its Aircraft* (New York: Orion Books, 1987), p. 42.

8. M. D. Klaas, *Last of the Flying Clippers: The Boeing B-314 Story* (Alglen, Pa.: Shiffer Publisher, Ltd., 1997), pp. 237–45.

9. Goodwin, p. 402.

10. Michael F. Reilly, as told to William J. Slocum, *Reilly of the White House* (New York: Simon & Schuster, 1947), p. 161.

11. Reilly, p. 188.

12. Gaither Littrell, "The VIP Express," *Flying* (September 1945), p. 26.

13. Ibid., p. 127.

14. Hamilton Fredericks, "The President's Pilot," *Flying* (May 1946), p. 108.

15. Merriman Smith, *Thank You, Mr. President: A White House Notebook by A. Merriman Smith* (New York: Da Capo Press, 1976), p. 34.

16. terHorst and Albertazzie, pp. 161–64.

17. Ibid., p. 163.

18. Dean Acheson, *Present at the Creation: My Years in the State Department* (New York: W. W. Norton & Company, 1969), p. 337.

19. Ibid., p. 488.

20. Ibid., p. 666.

21. terHorst and Albertazzie, pp. 171–74; William Manchester, *American Caesar:*

Douglas MacArthur, 1880–1964 (New York: Little, Brown and Company, 1978), pp. 585–97; David McCulloch, *Truman* (New York: Simon & Schuster, 1992), pp. 800–808.

22. terHorst and Albertazzie, p. 177.

23. Robert F. Dorr, *Air Force One* (St. Paul, Minn.: MBI Publishing Company, 2002), p. 45.

24. Ibid., pp. 50–51.

25. Dwight D. Eisenhower, *Waging Peace: The White House Years, 1956–1961* (New York: Doubleday, 1965), p. 415.

26. Michael R. Beschloss, *Mayday: Eisenhower, Khrushchev, and the U-2 Affair* (New York: Harper & Row, Publishers, 1986).

27. Leonid Kerber, *Stalin's Aviation Gulag: A Memoir of Andrei Tupolev and the Purge Era,* edited by Von Hardesty (Washington, D.C.: Smithsonian Institution Press, 1996), pp. 306–29.

28. William F. Reilly and William J. Slocum, *Reilly of the White House* (New York: Simon & Schuster, 1947), pp. 186–87.

29. terHorst and Albertazzie, pp. 156–57.

30. Ibid., p. 194.

31. Eisenhower, p. 438.

32. Nikita Khrushchev, *Khrushchev Remembers,* with an Introduction and Notes by Edward Crankshaw (Boston: Little, Brown and Company, 1970), p. 395.

33. terHorst and Albertazzie, pp. 196–98.

Chapter 3

1. Weinstein and Rubel, p. 555.

2. Glenn Porter, *Raymond Loewy: Designs for a Consumer Culture* (Wilmington, Delaware: Hagley Museum and Library, 2002), p. 124.

3. Paul Jodard, *Raymond Loewy* (New York: Taplinger Publishing Company, 1992), p. 155.

4. Ibid., p. 13.

5. Elizabeth Valk Long, "To Our Readers," *Time* (May 30, 1994), n.p.

6. Lawrence K. Altman and Todd S. Purdum, "In Kennedy File, a Portrait of Illness and Pain," *New York Times* (November 17, 2002), pp. 1, 28.

7. Rufus W. Youngblood, *20 Years in the Secret Service: My Life with Five*

Presidents (New York: Simon & Schuster, 1973), pp. 112–13.

8. Ibid., p. 117.

9. terHorst and Albertazzie, p. 211.

10. terHorst and Albertazzie, p. 121.

11. Lyndon Baines Johnson, *The Vantage Point: Perspectives on the Presidency 1963–1969* (New York: Holt, Rinehart and Winston, 1971), p. 12.

12. terHorst and Albertazzie, p. 217.

13. Merriman Smith, *Merriman Smith's Book of Presidents,* p. 210.

14. Ibid., pp. 210–11.

15. William Manchester, "A Troubled Flight from Dallas," *Look,* vol. 31, no. 4 (February 21, 1967), pp. 53–56.

16. Theodore White, *The Making of the President — 1964* (New York: Atheneum Publishers, 1965), p. 6.

17. Ibid., p. 7.

18. Dorr, p. 71.

19. terHorst and Albertazzie, p. 243.

20. Johnson, p. 363.

21. Frank Cormier, *LBJ The Way He Was* (Garden City, NY: Doubleday & Company, Inc., 1977), p. 248.

22. Cormier, p. 251.

23. Jack Valenti, *A Very Human President* (New York: W. W. Norton & Company, 1975), p. 282.

24. Cormier, p. 251.

25. *Look,* June 2, 1964, pp. 86–96.

26. Johnson, p. 379.

27. Cormier, p. 253.

28. Valenti, p. 285.

29. Cormier, p. 253.

30. Cormier, p. 254.

31. Cormier, p. 255.

Chapter 4

1. terHorst and Albertazzie, pp. 252–53.
2. Ibid., pp. 253–54.
3. Ibid.
4. Lou Cannon, "Nixon Flies West on Commercial Jet," *Washington Post* (December 27, 1973), pp. 1, A12.
5. terHorst and Albertazzie, pp. 278–95.
6. Richard Nixon, *The Memoirs of Richard Nixon* (New York: Grossett & Dunlap, 1978), p. 559.
7. terHorst and Albertazzie, pp. 307–11.
8. White, *The Making of the President — 1972* (New York: Atheneum Publishers: 1973), p. xi.
9. Nixon, p. 559.
10. White, pp. 6–7.
11. Bob Woodward and Carl Bernstein, *The Final Days* (New York: Simon & Schuster, 1976), p. 213.
12. Henry Kissinger, *Years of Upheaval* (Boston: Little, Brown and Company, 1982), p. 1132.
13. Nixon, p. 1090.
14. Gerald Ford, *A Time to Heal: The Autobiography of Gerald Ford* (Norwalk, Conn.: The Easton Press, 1979), p. 310.
15. Ibid.
16. Ibid., p. 311.
17. Ibid.
18. Ibid., pp. 311–12.
19. *San Francisco* (May 1983), vol. 25, p. 25.
20. Ford, p. 312.
21. Dorr, pp. 85–86.
22. Interviews with Bob Schieffer and Robert Pierpoint by author, May 1–2, 2003.
23. Hamilton Jordan, *Crisis: The Last Year of the Carter Presidency* (New York: G. P. Putnam's Sons, 1982), pp. 416–17.

Chapter 5

1. Lou Cannon, *President Reagan: The Role of a Lifetime* (New York: Simon & Schuster, 1991), p. 459.
2. Ibid., p. 460.
3. USAToday.com, "Air Force One Retired to Reagan Library," August 29, 2001. See http://www.usatoday.com/news/nation/2001/08/29/plane-retired.htm
4. Ronald Reagan, *An American Life* (New York: Simon & Schuster, 1990), p. 683.
5. Ibid., pp. 677–79.
6. Ibid., p. 679.

7. Harold Evans et al., *The American Century* (New York: Alfred A. Knopf, 1998), p. 647.
8. Pete Souza, *Unguarded Moments: Behind-the-Scenes Photographs of Ronald Reagan* (Fort Worth, Tex.: The Summit Group, 1992), pp. 50–56.
9. Nancy Reagan, with William Novak, *My Turn: The Memoirs of Nancy Reagan* (New York: Random House, 1989), p. 226.
10. John Hughes, "The Varied Ways of Knowing Reagan," *The Monitor* (October 20, 1999), p. 11. See http://www.csmonitor.com/durable/1999/10/20/fp11s2-csm.shtml
11. USS *Saratoga* Museum Foundation, "A Brief History of 'Marine One': The VH-3A Helicopter," undated. See http://www.saratogamuseum.org/events/VH3Ahistory.html
12. GlobalSecurity.org, "VH-3D Marine-1," undated.
13. CBSNews.com, "Marine One Flying High," September 18, 2002. See http://www.cbsnews.com/stories/2002/09/18/earlyshow/living/travel/main522391.shtml
14. Hughes.
15. Ibid.
16. Nancy Reagan, p. 368.
17. Bush, p. 121.
18. Joel Achenbach, "The Ultimate Perk," *Forbes FYI*, Winter 1996, pp. 117–18.
19. Andrew Rosenthal, "Air Force One Journal: 200,000 Miles Later, the President Gets His Wings," *New York Times* (September 9, 1990), p. A26.
20. Bush, p. 120.
21. *Flight International* (December 10, 2002), p. 15.
22. Dana Milbank, "White House Notebook," *Washington Post* (October 29, 1999), p. A19.
23. Bush, p. 121.
24. Ibid.
25. Ibid.
26. Michael Beschloss and Strobe Talbott, *At the Highest Levels: The Inside Story of the End of the Cold War* (Boston: Little, Brown, and Company, 1993), pp. 415–16.

Chapter 6

1. Todd Purdum, "On Air Force One, Cabin Fever," *New York Times* (November 12, 1995), p. E2.
2. GlobalSecurity.org, "VH-60 Marine-1," February 11, 2002.
3. Dee Dee Myers, Press Briefing, Office of the Press Secretary, The White House, May 20, 1993. See http://www.whitehouse.gov
4. George Larson, "Of Course You Realize Nothing Like This Could Never Happen," *Air & Space/Smithsonian* (August/September 1997), n.p. See http://www.airspacemag.com
5. John F. Harris and Steven Mufson, "A Presidential Face in the Crowd: Throngs of Aides and Journalists with Clinton in China Sets a Record," *Washington Post* (July 3, 1998), p. A30.
6. Ibid.
7. John M. Broder, "In the Land of a Billion, A Fitting Presidential Retinue," *New York Times* (June 21, 1998), Week in Review, p. 5.
8. "Clinton Stays Longer than Planned," Champaign *News-Gazette* (January 28, 1998); Paul Wood, "No Discipline for Air Force One Crew after Williard," Champaign *News-Gazette* (May 19, 1998), n.p. See http://www.news-gazette.com/theprez_mud.html and http://www.news-gazette.com/ngsearch/story.cfm?number=2769
9. CBSNews.com, "Bush on 9/11: Moment to Moment," September 12, 2002. See http://www.cbsnews.com/stories/2002/09/11/60II/main521718.shtml
10. Ibid.
11. Ibid.
12. John M. Donnelly, "Air Force One, How Do You Read?" *White House Weekly*, September 17, 2002.
13. Office of the Prime Minister, Public Relations Department, "The Government Aircraft." See www.kantei.go.jp/foreign/vt2/main/07/photo-senyoki01.html
14. "Putin awaits his 'Air Force One,'" BBC News, May 11, 2002. See http://news.bbc.co.uk/2/hi/not_in_website/syndication/monitoring/media_reports/1981091.stm
15. Heiko Stolzke, "The 'Flugbereitschaft' of the German Ministry of Defence,"

Flug Revue (April 2001). See http://www.flug-revue.rotor.com
16. CBSNews.com, p. 6.
17. Ibid.
18. CBSNews.com, pp. 5–6.
19. William B. Scott, "F-16 Pilots Considered Ramming Flight 93," *Aviation Week & Space Technology* (September 9, 2002), pp. 71–74.
20. CBSNews.com, p. 6.
21. Mike Allen, "White House Drops Claim of Threat to Bush," *Washington Post* (September 27, 2001), p. A8.
22. Elisabeth Bumiller, "War Movies and Face Time: Welcome Aboard Air Force One," *International Herald Tribune* (October 30, 2002), n.p. See http://www.iht.com/articles/75228.html
23. Ibid.
24. Charles R. Babcock, "Campaigning via Air Force One: Public Foots Much of the Bill," *Washington Post* (December 31, 1991), p. A15. Richard S. Dunham, "Air Force One: Now It's Bush's Weapon," *Business Week* (May 13, 2002). See http://www.businessweek.com/bwdaily/dnflash/may2002/nf20020513_1049.htm
25. Bumiller.
26. Ibid.
27. Weinstein and Rubel, p. 659.
28. Cullen Murphy, "Back to Basics," *The Atlantic* (December 1998).
29. "Final Flight for Retiring 'Air Force One' 707," CNNfyi, August 30, 2001. See http://www.cnn.com/2001/ALLPOLITICS/08/29/bush.plane/index.html
30. "Plans Lift Hilltop Library Up a Level," *Ventura County Star* (March 10, 2002), p. B9.
31. United States Air Force Museum Presidential Aircraft Gallery. See http://www.wpafb.af.mil/museum/annex/ans.html
32. Steven Thomma, "Boeing 707 That Served Presidents from Kennedy to Clinton Makes Final Flight to Museum," Knight-Ridder News Service, May 16, 1998. See http://www.acorn.net/JFKplace/11/11-18/11-18-06html

Index

Credits

TEHABI BOOKS

NORTHWORD

Tehabi Books conceived, designed, and produced *Air Force One* and has conceived and produced many award-winning books that are recognized for their strong narrative and visual content. Tehabi works with national and international publishers, corporations, institutions, and nonprofit groups to identify, develop, and implement comprehensive publishing programs. Tehabi is located in San Diego, California. www.tehabi.com

PRESIDENT AND PUBLISHER: Chris Capen
VICE PRESIDENT OF OPERATIONS: Sam Lewis
DIRECTOR, CORPORATE MARKETING: Martha Remmell
DIRECTOR, CORPORATE PUBLISHING: Chris Brimble
CORPORATE SALES MANAGER: Andrew Arias

SENIOR ART DIRECTOR: John Baxter
PRODUCTION ARTIST: Mark Santos
PICTURE RESEARCHER: Mary Beth Farlow

EDITOR: Garrett Brown
RESEARCHER AND CONSULTING EDITOR: Gene Eisman
EDITORIAL ASSISTANT: Katie Franco

COPY EDITOR: Lisa Wolff
PROOFREADER: Jacqueline Garrett
INDEXER: Ken DellaPenta

Tehabi Books offers special discounts for bulk purchases for sales promotions and use as premiums. Specific, large-quantity needs can be met with special editions, custom covers, and by repurposing existing materials. For information, contact Andrew Arias, corporate sales manager, at Tehabi Books, 4920 Carroll Canyon Road, Suite 200, San Diego, California 92121; or, by telephone, at (800) 243-7259.

Library of Congress Cataloging-in-Publication Data

Hardesty, Von, 1939–
    Air Force One : the aircraft that shaped the modern presidency / by Von Hardesty ; foreword by Bob Schieffer.
        p. cm.
    Includes biographical references and index.
    ISBN 1-55971-894-3
    1. Air Force One (Presidential aircraft). 2. Air Force One (Airplanes). 3. Boeing 747 (Jet transports). 4. Presidents—Transportation—United States. 5. Presidents—Protection—United States. I. Title.

TL723.H37 2003
387.7'42'088351—dc21

2003055197

First Edition
Printed through Dai Nippon Printing Co., Ltd., in Korea
10 9 8 7 6 5 4 3 2 1

NorthWord Press is an imprint of Creative Publishing international (CPi). NorthWord publishes many of America's finest nature photographers and illustrators and has a growing line of children's fiction and educational books.

PRESIDENT AND CEO: Michael Eleftheriou
VICE PRESIDENT AND PUBLISHER: Linda Ball
VICE PRESIDENT, RETAIL SALES AND DEVELOPMENT: Kevin Haas
EXECUTIVE EDITOR: Bryan Trandem

For information, write to:
Creative Publishing international, Inc.
18705 Lake Drive East
Chanhassen, Minnesota 55317
www.creativepub.com

Captions

PAGE 2: President George W. Bush and First Lady Laura Bush wave as they enter Air Force One at the Arkansas Regional Airport on November 4, 2002. Bush was on the last day of a marathon campaign trip that took him to fifteen states and seventeen cities.

PAGE 4: President George W. Bush made a seven-day, four-country trip to Europe in May 2002. The president walks up the steps of Air Force One after his twenty-six hour sojourn in France, a stop that included a special memorial service at the United States war cemetery at Normandy.

PAGE 6: Air Force One lands at Lambert–St. Louis International Airport in St. Louis, Missouri, on March 17, 1996.

PAGE 192: Lyn Nugent, President Johnson's grandson, makes an important telephone call on board Air Force One on December 15, 1968.

A Note on the Type

This book was composed using the typefaces Monotype Ehrhardt for text and Hoefler Knockout for captions and display.

Ehrhardt is derived from types believed to have been cut by Nicholas Kis, a Hungarian punch-cutter who worked in Amsterdam in 1686. In 1938, the Monotype Type Drawing Offices, under the direction of scholar Stanley Morison, introduced the modern version of the face. Morison used specimen pages from the 1739 catalog of the Hr. Erhardt Foundry in Leipzig as a model. The typeface was modified to improve legibility and introduce uniformity. Monotype has since adapted the face to digital format.

Knockout is an extension of the typeface Champion Gothic, designed by Hoefler Type Foundry. Champion Gothic offered designers a modern translation of the wood-type headline faces used in American theatre handbills, music sheets, and posters in the early twentieth-century. Knockout consists of thirty-two variations of the Champion Gothic face, appropriate for body text.